Mass Customization: An Enterprise-Wide Business Strategy

How Build to Order, Assemble to Order, Configure to Order, Make to Order, and Engineer to Order Manufacturers Increase Profits and Better Satisfy Customers

David J. Gardner

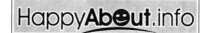

20660 Stevens Creek Blvd., Suite 210
Cupertino, CA 95014

Copyright © 2009 by David J. Gardner

First Printing: May 2009
Paperback ISBN: 978-1-60005-146-3 (1-60005-146-4)
Place of Publication: Silicon Valley, California USA
Paperback Library of Congress Number: 2009927452

eBook ISBN: 978-1-60005-147-0 (1-60005-147-2)

Trademarks

All terms mentioned in this book that are known to be trademarks or service marks have been appropriately capitalized. Happy About® cannot attest to the accuracy of this information. Use of a term in this book should not be regarded as affecting the validity of any trademark or service mark.

Warning and Disclaimer

Every effort has been made to make this book as complete and as accurate as possible, but no warranty of fitness is implied. The information provided is on an "as is" basis. The authors and the publisher shall have neither liability nor responsibility to any person or entity with respect to loss or damages arising from the information contained in this book.

A Message from Happy About®

Thank you for your purchase of this Happy About book. It is available online at http://www.happyabout.info/mass-customization.php or at other online and physical bookstores.

- Please contact us for quantity discounts at sales@happyabout.info
- If you want to be informed by e-mail of upcoming Happy About® books, please e-mail bookupdate@happyabout.info

Happy About is interested in you if you are an author who would like to submit a non-fiction book proposal or a corporation that would like to have a book written for you. Please contact us by e-mail editorial@happyabout.info or phone (1-408-257-3000).

Other Happy About books available include:

- Overcoming Inventoritis
  http://www.happyabout.info/overcoming-inventoritis.php
- 42 Rules for Growing Enterprise Revenue
  http://www.happyabout.info/42rules/growing-enterprise-revenue.php
- Expert Product Management
  http://www.happyabout.info/expertproductmanagement.php
- Scrappy Project Management
  http://www.happyabout.info/scrappyabout/project-management.php
- The Business Rule Revolution
  http://www.happyabout.info/business-rule-revolution.php
- Climbing the Ladder of Business Intelligence
  http://www.happyabout.info/climbing-ladder.php
- Marketing Campaign Development
  http://www.happyabout.info/marketingcampaigndevelopment.php
- I'm on Facebook—Now What???
  http://www.happyabout.info/facebook.php
- I'm on LinkedIn—Now What???
  http://www.happyabout.info/linkedinhelp.php
- 42 Rules for 24 Hour Success on LinkedIn
  http://www.happyabout.info/42rules/24hr-success-linkedin.php
- Twitter Means Business
  http://www.happyabout.info/twitter/tweet2success.php
- Marketing Thought
  http://www.happyabout.info/MarketingThought.php

Dedication

I want to acknowledge the love and support of my family who have encouraged me to create this book for many years including my wife, Nancy; my father, Robert Gardner; my late mother, Patricia Gardner; my sister, Deborah and my brother, Brian. Thank you. I'm most grateful.

Acknowledgments

Mark Joyner, in his book *The Irresistible Offer*, offers the following thought on his acknowledgment page:

> When an author lists only his name on the cover of his work, it is really an exercise in ego and ungratefulness. Without the help of a great many people, this book would not be at all possible.

Mark, I know what you mean. In particular, I want to acknowledge Robert W. Duncan, Kevin Kalkhoven, Durwin Wright, Bruce Crawford, Guy Gandenberger, B. Joseph Pine, Dr. David Anderson, Harold Pinto, Jay Abraham, and Dr. Alan Weiss. Thank you.

I want to give special acknowledgement to B. Joseph Pine whom I have had the distinct pleasure of personally knowing since 1999. His pioneering book, Mass Customization: The New Frontier in Business Competition, was the first work that so comprehensively detailed the opportunity mass customization represents and its significance in our evolution. It remains the "gold standard." His insights continue to be invaluable to me and the business world.

I'm especially grateful to Dr. Frank Piller for writing the foreword to this book. We've known each other for a number of years but have only corresponded via e-mail. I look forward to meeting Dr. Piller in person in the near future. We are kindred spirits in the mass customization field.

This book likely would not have been created were it not for Mitchell Levy and Happy About. Mitchell contacted me back in January 2007 and asked if I would be interested in creating a book about mass customization. I am so delighted he did. Mitchell and his team have been fantastic to work with. Thank you, Mitchell.

I've enjoyed working with many clients including manufacturers, companies involved in creating and offering product configurator technology and consulting services, and clients who have asked me to deliver keynote addresses on mass customization. Each situation created opportunities to enhance my understanding. It's not possible to get a degree in mass customization. My knowledge has come from solving real business problems without the benefit of a roadmap or step-by-step procedures. My mass customization education has been, of necessity, hands-on working in the trenches. It has also come as a result of my passion for conquering the challenges that plague manufacturers of configurable products.

Contents

Foreword by Frank T. Piller

Today's pressing global economic crisis is putting efficiency and cost-cutting back on the agenda of executives and entrepreneurs worldwide. Yet, cost cuts should not be blindly pursued at the risk of damaging the long-term strategy and value proposition of an organization. Firms pursuing differentiation strategies do not have to turn themselves into cost leaders; what they must be able to do is offer better, cheaper, and simpler differentiation through the creation of a unique portfolio of products and services for each of their customers or groups of customers.

Mass customization is a key strategy to meet this challenge. The term denotes an offering that meets the demands of each individual customer, but that still can be produced with the efficiency of mass production. Or, as B. Joseph Pine, who made mass customization popular with his 1992 book, Mass Customization: The New Frontier in Business Competition, recently said: "Today I define Mass Customization as the low-cost, high-volume, efficient production of individually customized offerings."

In other words, the goal is to provide customers what they want when they want it. Consider the following examples as positive examples of mass customization. BMW customers can use an online toolkit to design the roof of a Mini Cooper with their very own graphics or picture, which is then reproduced with an advanced digital printing system on a special foil. The toolkit has enabled BMW to tap into the custom after-sales market, which was previously owned by niche companies. In addition, Mini Cooper customers can also choose from among hundreds of options for many of the car's components, as BMW is able to manufacture all cars on-demand according to each buyer's individual order.

Another great example of mass customization is American Power Conversion (APC), a case described by Lars Hvam in a special case study issue of the *International Journal of Mass Customization* (2006). APC sells, designs, produces, delivers, and installs large complex infrastructure systems for data centers, and components for these systems. At the heart of the mass customization strategy of this company is a module-based product range and the use of product configuration systems for sales and order processing. In addition, the company has implemented a manufacturing concept, which involves the mass production of standard components in the Far East, and customer order-based final assembly at various production sites around the world within close customer proximity. The results of applying mass customization principles included a reduction of the overall delivery time for a complete system from around 400 days to only 16 days. Production costs were also significantly reduced. At the same time, the company's capability to introduce new products has increased dramatically. Due to the modular system architecture, new component technologies can be integrated within a matter of days and not months, as was the case before.

What do these examples have in common? Regardless of product category or industry, they have all turned customers' heterogeneous needs into an opportunity to create value, rather than a problem to be minimized, challenging the "one-size-fits-all" assumption of traditional mass production. The concept of mass customization makes business sense in these times. Why wouldn't people want to be treated as individual customers, with products tailored to their specific needs? But mass customization has been trickier to implement than first anticipated. There is still a large lack of knowledge about how to apply mass customization in practice.

This is where David Gardner's experience comes to the fore. In this book, David has summarized his vast experience in implementing the elements of a sustainable and profitable mass customization system in diverse business settings. He is one of the few individuals in the world that really have researched and executed mass customization thinking in a consistent and pragmatic way. So I am sure that you will benefit tremendously from his advice and reflections to better understand how you can build for your company a full set of mass customization capabilities that will set your business ahead in these tough times.

Frank T. Piller,
Codirector, MIT Smart Customization Group,
MIT, USA
Professor of Management,
RWTH Aachen University, Germany
www.mass-customization.de

Introduction

I've been helping manufacturers implement mass customization since the early 1980s—before the expression "mass customization" was coined by Stan Davis in his best-selling book *Future Perfect* back in 1987. There has been much written about mass customization as a high-level business strategy but far less written about actually implementing mass customization within a manufacturing company.

Some would suggest that you merely need to purchase product configurator software and, voilà, you're in the mass customization business. Hogwash! This would be tantamount to suggesting one can write a great sales letter merely because you have Microsoft Word.

Mass customization is not a departmental challenge nor is it an IT challenge. Mass customization must be approached holistically across the enterprise and even out to the extended enterprise to your dealers and customers. This book will help you understand why this is the case.

In his book *The Strategy Paradox*, Michael Raynor offers the following key insights:

• Companies spend 95% of their energy getting the product and technology right.

- As a consequence, there is little capacity to look at the "business model" question.

Make no mistake about it:

Mass customization is a business model question.

Companies with highly configurable products that thrive in their marketplace need to combine the technical superiority of their products with operational excellence. They need to be able to seamlessly connect the customer to all organizations in the enterprise so the hand-offs from organization to organization resemble the efficiency of an aircraft carrier flight deck.

If your company continually experiences the pain of not being able to seamlessly connect the customer to the enterprise and efficiently drive the order demand across the enterprise, your business is not set up properly. There is a misalignment between what your company needs and what you have.

In company after company, I've seen very bright people work months or years to solve the operational challenges associated with highly customized products without success. It's not merely a matter of buying product configurator software—it's a matter of setting up your entire business to accommodate your highly configurable products.

Who should read this book?

- Anyone who's company faces a constant, uphill challenge with respect to quoting, configuring, and producing highly configured products.
- Anyone who has made an investment in product configurator software and wants to understand why operational efficiencies and profits haven't improved.
- Anyone who would like to get a better understanding of what is required to implement mass customization and the power mass customization has to transform certain industries.

This book has been prepared with discrete manufacturers—companies that produce a product that you can physically touch—in mind. The principles of mass customization can be applied in services (professional, insurance, and financial), process manufacturing, and other industries, but I'll not be touching on those areas.

1 Why Manufacturers Can't Ignore It

Dell changed the competitive landscape by

- Offering customized products directly to customers on demand without premiums in either price or lead time
- Minimizing inventory to unthinkable levels—more than 100 inventory turns per year
- Being agile—quickly responding to the market/technology changes
- Eliminating the cost and risk of finished goods inventory
- Successfully executing a mass customization strategy quarter after quarter, year after year

Did Michael Dell adopt a mass customization business strategy because he believed it would provide a magical path to build his business empire? No.

Michael Dell adopted mass customization for far more pragmatic reasons. From his humble college dorm room, he could only *afford* to build products on demand. He didn't have the resources (capital, work space, infrastructure, etc.) to build finished goods inventory and put it on a shelf in the hope that someone would come along and buy what he had built. He could only *afford* to produce real customer orders. Michael Dell was forced into this business strategy due to tangible constraints, not because he recognized the larger potential of the mass customization business strategy.

Increasingly, manufacturers covet the success that mass customizers like Dell achieved up through the 2004 period when revenues hit $49 billion with profits of $3 billion.[1] Internet-based commerce and mass customization have created new expectations in the marketplace and new demands for manufacturers. Manufacturers of configurable products must rapidly transition to a mass customization business strategy and, as a consequence, become lean, agile, and Internet-accessible.

Current information technology and business methodologies are based on an outdated paradigm: Mass Production. This paradigm prevents mass customizers from implementing a successful Internet-based commerce strategy.

Savvy executives are beginning to realize that the millions of dollars invested in implementing sophisticated enterprise resource planning (ERP) systems have failed to provide any competitive advantage. They will soon come to understand that ERP has its roots in mass production, an increasingly irrelevant business strategy that conflicts with twenty-first century customer needs and expectations. And, these same executives will be looking closely at companies like Dell to find a more relevant and effective business strategy—a strategy called "mass customization."

> Mass customization is more than just a manufacturing process, logistics system or marketing strategy. It could well be the organizing principle of business in the next century, just as mass production was the organizing principle in this one. (*Fortune*, September 29, 1998, pp. 115–116)

Fortune magazine is correct—mass customization is the organizing principle for twenty-first century manufacturers. Manufacturers must adopt

---

1. Dell has veered from its core mass customization strategy in recent years and stumbled in the marketplace and with its shareholders. In the context of this book, Dell is used to illustrate the mass customization business model and its potential, not as a model of how a company should define and execute a larger product and distribution strategy.

the following beliefs to transition to a mass customization business strategy:

- Mass customization and Internet-based commerce will revolutionize the twenty-first century economy just as mass production revolutionized the twentieth-century economy.

- Mass customization and Internet-based commerce are inextricably linked—Internet-based commerce demands that customers interact *directly* with a manufacturer.

- Mass customization must be addressed as an enterprise-wide business strategy, not a series of departmental challenges.

- ERP offerings such as SAP and Oracle are optimized for mass production, not mass customization; new technology that augments ERP is required to support mass customization.

- Add-on applications to ERP such as sales configurators do not solve the problem as they are focused on departmental solutions, not an enterprise-wide solution.

The Business Imperative

Manufacturers that thrive and prosper in the twenty-first century must treat customers as "insiders." Under mass customization, the customer is an "insider." The customer can purchase products that match their needs. The customer can select from an array of choices.

Conversely, under mass production, the customer is an "outsider." The customer is limited to getting products the manufacturer produces and offers through its distribution channel. While mass-produced products can be instantly available (if they are in stock), they often fall short of the customer's needs.

The connection between customer and manufacturer must be seamless. Customers won't have the manufacturer's salespeople acting as an ombudsman on their behalf to get their quotes or orders processed. Customers need to be able to determine what configurations are available, what price they will pay, and when they can expect delivery. Manufacturers must adopt mass customization as an enterprise-wide business strategy to

- Link customers and configuration capability directly to the enterprise via the Internet
- Set expectations about what configurations can be produced
- Increase customer satisfaction and loyalty
- Reduce time-to-market
- Reduce internal costs to support evolving product offerings
- Decrease order cycle time
- Reduce the cost of documenting products
- Eliminate artificial product constraints due to effort/complexity to modify or enhance a product line
- Eliminate cost of configuration errors
- Increase flexibility and responsiveness to "give customers what they want"
- Reduce overhead
- Eliminate the costs associated with "specials"

Manufacturer's Dilemma

Customers no longer accept a "one-size-fits-all" solution. Customers want what they want, when they want it, and at a competitive price. The dilemma facing manufacturers is illustrated by Henry Ford's statement: "You can have it in any color you want as long as it's black."

The implication behind Mr. Ford's statement is quite profound for mass producers: *The efficiencies that reduce a manufacturer's costs cannot be achieved if you allow variations in products.*

Mass customization is the antithesis of mass production. There has been an exponential increase in customer expectations about what manufacturers should produce. This has contributed to corresponding increases in the complexity of product design, production, selling, and service. To manage this complexity, companies must deploy systems and processes optimized for mass customization. Here's why.

The cornerstone of an ERP system (and the mass production paradigm) is the bill of materials—the list of ingredients required to build a product. Mass producers create a top assembly bill of material for each order configuration. Even the most minor changes in a customer's order configuration mandate the creation of a new top assembly bill of material. This fact, of course, requires engineering's expertise and knowledge, consumes scarce engineering resources, and increases order cycle time.

As more and more order configurations are needed, the burden to create, support, and maintain additional top assembly bills of material grows exponentially, particularly when new options or enhancements are created. While the process of creating top assembly bill of materials is efficient when there are a limited number of configurations, it has dire impacts if each order configuration must be documented. This problem is compounded when you realize this effort will likely have no benefit for any future orders.

Under mass production, marketing decides what product configurations will be offered, engineering designs and documents these configurations, and manufacturing builds the varying configurations and puts them in finished good inventory for subsequent sale to a customer or distributor. When order configurations come in that have not previously been documented, engineering must document the new configuration.

Under mass customization, engineering defines the configuration possibilities in the form of reusable knowledge based on product modularity, marketing decides which configuration possibilities will be offered to customers by filtering engineering's knowledge, and manufacturing builds configurations derived from the customer's use of this shared knowledge immediately after order receipt. Engineering defines additional knowledge to integrate new features and options.

Under mass customization, (1) configuration knowledge is captured, reused, and leveraged across the enterprise; (2) a bill of material and engineering resources are not needed for each order configuration unless a new feature or option is needed; and (3) the customer's order requirements are mapped directly into manufacturing. Under mass production, these efficiencies are impossible.

Transitioning to Mass Customization

Adopting mass customization as a business strategy will have a profound and positive effect on an enterprise. Mass customization is not a departmental problem; it must be approached on an enterprise-wide basis.

It affects sales, marketing, order administration, engineering, manufacturing, service, and, most importantly, your customers.

Twenty-first century customers will not "settle" for what a manufacturer produces. Mass customization ensures that customers won't be forced to "settle." It also ensures that the challenge of "giving customers what they want" can be met efficiently and cost-effectively.

2 Mass Customization Defined

Within the manufacturing world, mass customization is about producing highly configured products with the efficiency of a mass-produced product. Mass customization is also commonly referred to as

- Build to order
- Assemble to order
- Configure to order
- Make to order
- Engineer to order

Please note the use of the repetitive phrase "to order." This is important. "To order" implies that configured products are made on the basis of an actual order—it is the order that drives the order demand, not a finished goods forecast.

Contrasting mass production with the mass customization paradigm, under mass production, everything about a product is predictable—except for the demand. When a product is produced under the mass production paradigm, there generally is no order—the product is produced based on a forecast. There is no customer at this point. The product has been previously engineered, a detailed bill of material has been created, prototypes built, and (hopefully) all the bugs and kinks associated with mass producing the product have been worked out prior to going to the marketplace. Any issues related to variation in product configuration have been worked out ahead of time, e.g., color schemes. A customer has no ability to influence the ultimate product that is made available for sale—the customer is merely presented with choices in the retail marketplace.

Some manufacturing companies offer highly customized products under what is referred to as an "engineer-to-order" business paradigm. This means that individual order configurations require significant engineering effort to literally engineer and document the product so the each order configuration can be produced. In some instances, the cost of the engineering effort is born by the customer; in most, it is not.

Mass customization assumes that the engineering effort associated with designing and modularizing a product line has been completed long before an order is accepted. A key, underlying assumption in mass customization is that the company is not hand-crafting individual order configurations. All the engineering and planning concerning what to offer the customer has been made ahead of time to improve the efficiency of producing the customer's order.

I favor an approach I refer to as "customer-driven manufacturing (CDM)." This is an integrated business process for transitioning to mass customization. CDM is focused around the way your customers and sales organization think about your products. The four key aspects of a CDM effort involve

- Bill of material (or product) structure modularization
- Configurator tool development
- Business process integration
- Training

By aligning your bill of material structure in the way customers and your sales team think about the configurability of your products, you eliminate the interpretation errors that often occur during order entry or in the factory. Imagine the efficiencies associated with sales, engineering, marketing, and manufacturing operating with exactly the same understanding of product line. And because the CDM approach is adopted to better serve your customers, it is far easier to get everyone to embrace such an initiative.

If a manufacturing company is organized to easily accommodate highly customized order configurations across the entire enterprise, great efficiencies can be realized. What does "efficiency" mean?

A company needs to be able to seamlessly drive the business from "quote-to-cash" without incurring multiple rework steps, what I refer to as "start/ stop, start/stop." There has to be a steady flow of progress from the time a quote is generated until the time the cash is collected rather than experiencing a series of rework loops.

From silos to seamless

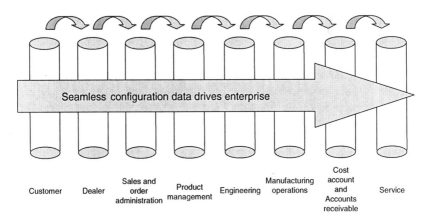

| Customer | Dealer | Sales and order administration | Product management | Engineering | Manufacturing operations | Cost account and Accounts receivable | Service |

If a manufacturing company is not set up to seamlessly offer and produce highly customized products to customer expectations, great inefficiencies result that can compromise the financial performance of the business:

- A $1 billion manufacturing company offering highly customized capital equipment generates an operating profit of about 1%.
- Fire/rescue vehicle manufacturers must offer highly customized vehicles yet have low, single-digit operating profits (if they have any profit at all). Some profits stem solely from vehicle financing, not from operations. Quite a few of the top 10 North American fire/rescue vehicle manufacturers have been in or are on the verge of bankruptcy.

Mass Customization   11

- Boeing and Airbus have been at the mercy of a galley manufacturer to produce highly configured galleys tailored to each airline customers needs. Late deliveries of the galleys have resulted in late deliveries of aircraft and delayed revenue recognition. In-process aircraft have had to be pulled off the production line to wait for the galleys creating operational challenges about getting the aircraft back into the production slots.

Dell produces computers built to order. They provide an array of products and clearly explain to their customers what option choices the customer can select from to tailor the product to individual needs.

Dell does a really terrific job. Dell is organized to easily accommodate customized products across the enterprise and the extended enterprise.

What would happen if the Dell product configurator offered configurations that the factory could not produce? Orders would get backed up, customers would have to be notified that the order configuration they placed cannot be built, pricing would change, and the delivery of the end-product would be delayed. In short, chaos would ensue.

Sadly, most companies with configurable products don't have the level of seamlessness and transparency with their customers that Dell does. And, as a result, they routinely experience the problems described above.

Operational Challenges with Highly Configurable Products

Here are some observations that I've made about operational challenges many companies experience with configurable products:

- Engineering is overwhelmed supporting individual order demand.
- Manufacturing lacks the ability to efficiently produce individual orders:

Mass Customization Defined

- Reliance on "tribal knowledge."
- Lack of assembly procedure documentation.
- Items missing in bill of materials discovered during manufacturing process.

- The product (bill of material) structure needs to be simplified and flattened:

  - The product structure must be "add-only." All too often, the product structure is defined at too high a level meaning that parts and sub-assemblies are often actually deleted in customer configurations only to add others. This overstates order costing and adversely impacts inventory control.

  - The product structure all too often is incorrect in terms of supporting the customer's actual order configuration requirements.

- The customer order configuration process is "people-dependent" rather than "process-dependent" exposing the company to great risk. Too much tribal knowledge is required to configure and produce customer orders. Too much hand-holding is needed to get orders processed through the organization and out to the customer.

- Orders that are not fully configured are prematurely loaded to the backlog causing no end of difficulties related to booking and de-booking orders which compounds production control's challenge of understanding what is viable in the backlog.

- Customers purchase systems yet receive key components of the ultimate system causing receiving difficulties and challenges reconciling invoices so payments can be made. This is often due to components being shipped from different physical locations and arriving at different points in time.

- Too much critical business information is driven and supported outside normal ERP system in Word and Excel documents, e.g., quotations, forecasting, invoicing, finished goods inventory transactions, packing lists, backlog management, and price lists. There is no systematic, holistic approach to managing all of this interrelated data.

- When people experience problems, they work around them rather than initiate corrective action to prevent the reoccurrence. This is particularly troublesome when new employees take over someone's existing responsibilities or when someone leaves the company.

- Frustration and employee burnout is high—this could result in a high employee turnover rate which could threaten company growth.
- Customer frustration grows.
- The sales team is so busy chasing details associated with getting orders booked and the backlog of orders produced that prospective customers must wait and wait for someone to attend to their needs; business is lost to competition.

In essence, most organizations are reactive, choosing to wait for problems to occur so they can be corrected. Dr. Alan Weiss offers the following insights and a diagram from his book, *The Great Big Book of Process Visuals*:

> There is an over-emphasis on problem solving usually at the expense of innovation. If people are constantly trying to fix things, then they are seldom trying to improve things. And most organizations reward the former and penalize the latter (since it's somewhat risky). I use this graphic to demonstrate the difference between the two pursuits.

The first diagram below represents "problem solving" or "firefighting" while the second considers the impact of "innovation" in resolving an issue.

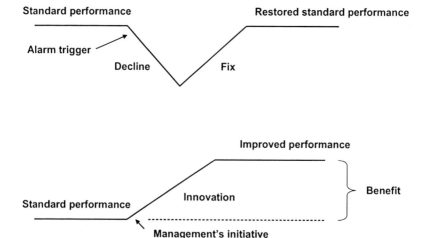

Dr. Weiss suggests that companies seldom have even a 50/50 ratio between problem solving and innovation adopting more of a 95/5 ratio in favor of problem solving. If a company only concerns itself with fixing problems, the company doesn't get any better. Innovation is required to improve performance.

Many years ago, the chief operating officer (COO) of a company wanted my assistance to help resolve a product configurability problem that he alleged was "killing my company." After investing a modest amount of time with his team, I concluded they weren't serious about resolving their issues and declined the opportunity to assist them. It was only after the third call from the COO that I (reluctantly) offered to do a small project. I should have followed my instincts. The people in the company loved fighting fires. As I anticipated, I could not get people's attention to work on a solution. The COO repeatedly cancelled meetings to discuss the situation as "something came up." The company ended up losing their biggest customer—a customer who represented more than 80% of the company's revenue as it failed to come to grips with its biggest challenge: product configurability.

While this may be an extreme example, it is more representative of the norm than one might think.

Mass Customization Defined

3 The Evolution to Mass Customization

The diagram below illustrates the gradual evolution to mass customization:

Evolution to mass customization

Nineteenth century	Twentieth century	Twenty-first century

Craft Production

Craft production offered customers what they wanted but at a price: long lead times and difficulty getting additional units "just like the first one." In today's world, one would think that craft production resides solely within the province of artisans. Yet, some industrial product manufacturers employ craft production techniques, e.g., no tooling and hand-fitting of assemblies. This production technique makes the product difficult to support as parts aren't defined in engineering drawings and therefore aren't always "interchangeable." It is difficult to achieve great efficiency under a craft production paradigm.

Mass Production

Mass production offers great economies but brought with it the challenge of not being able to support much in terms of variety. Everything had to be the same to promote the greatest manufacturing efficiencies which enabled the lowest possible price. As Henry Ford said, "You can have it any color you want as long as it's black." Why?

The introduction of any variability within the manufacturing process introduced inefficiency that would increase cost. Henry Ford believed that the customer was willing to sacrifice personal preferences to have the lowest cost. And, for some time, he was right, until competition evolved offering color as a choice. All of a sudden, the choice of color was no longer optional—the marketplace liked and preferred the opportunity to make a choice. However, to produce products of different colors, the underlying assumption would have had to be that this would be a source of competitive advantage and differentiation though it would not allow for significant premiums in pricing.

Mass production has a solid grip in the manufacturing world. It's not going away. Most of the products found in Home Depot, Target, Wal-Mart, Macy's, grocery stores, cell phones, toasters, coffee pots, and clothing and apparel are mass produced. It is unlikely that this will change much over time unless there is a need for premium products with premium pricing that warrant such offerings.

Engineer-to-Order

Under this scenario, there is a high level of engineering content and effort required for each order configuration. Sometimes there is compensation for this engineering effort; in non-governmental applications, there usually is no compensation.

For example, if the U.S. Air Force contracts for a new fighter plane, they may well pay for the engineering effort and a few prototypes to evaluate the efficacy of the design before the plane is put into a mass production environment. The prototypes may involve craft production techniques in the absence of hard tooling and other items that promote manufacturing efficiency.

Engineer-to-order is also found in commercial products. For example, for customized fire/rescue vehicles, the cost of engineering the vehicle is generally not recoverable from the customer as the customizations are considered a manufacturer's "cost of doing business" by the customer. Why? There are enough manufacturers willing to do what a customer wants at no additional charge just to win the business from the customer. This creates a "dog-eat-dog" environment where low margins usually result.

Mass Customization

Under this scenario, the engineering work has been done in advance of the orders being placed in terms of carefully laying out what options and capabilities are available to the customer.

This isn't to say there aren't "specials" or enhancements to the product offerings aren't sometimes required to support the order demand. It does suggest, however, that the bulk of the engineering work—the pre-engineering and product modularization—is done in advance of an order being taken. This allows for the modules to be recomposed into individual customer order configurations with little or no involvement from engineering.

Is mass customization going to replace mass production? No. There are situations where mass production is appropriate and will continue to be appropriate.

In general, there may be an opportunity for mass producers to offer mass-customized products where there is a need to differentiate and customers are willing to pay a premium for such customizations.

At stores like Home Depot, a customer can order special kitchen cabinets as per the customer's individualized requirements. To produce these orders at low cost requires mass customization practices be employed by the manufacturers offering such products.

Contrasting the Strategies

	Mass Production	Engineer-to-Order	Mass Customization
Driving force for order configurations	Marketing and retailers	Customer	Customer
Distribution	Retailers	Direct to customer or dealer	Direct to customer or dealer
Bill of material needs	Very accurate order configuration bill of material	Very accurate order configuration bill of material	Order bill of material derived from customer order
Level of engineering effort in each order configuration	Heavy upfront effort	Heavy upfront effort	Limited or no engineering effort

Mass Production

We see that a company's marketing department and the retailers are the driving force behind the order configurations that are offered to the customer. They, in effect, determine what the customer is going to see in the marketplace. The customer has no direct involvement in what is available.

Distribution of products is handled through the retail sales channel. The engineering effort needs to be quite precise as the manufacturer will build lots of units for each order configuration offered—this requires a lot of effort upfront on the part of engineering.

Engineer-to-Order

Under this business paradigm, the customer is the driving force behind the order configuration. Often, products are purchased according to detailed requirements specifications enumerating all the salient points of the product to be produced.

Distribution of products offered under this paradigm usually directly to the customer or through a dealer who represents the manufacturer.

The engineering effort needs to be quite precise as manufacturing needs to know exactly what is required to produce the product. If critical items are inadvertently left off the bill of material, it will not be until very late in the process that someone identifies the gap.

Mass Customization

Under this business paradigm, the customer is the driving force behind each order configuration. Just as in the engineer-to-order business paradigm, products can be purchased according to detailed requirements specifications enumerating all the salient points of the product to be produced or from a product configurator tool that enumerates the choices a customer makes.

Distribution of products offered under this paradigm usually occurs directly to the customer or through a dealer who represents the manufacturer.

Under mass customization, there is a significant effort upfront to engineer the essential features of the product and determine how different modules can be recomposed into specific order configurations. The big difference, however, is that, unless some new order requirement surfaces, engineering does not need to get bogged down in creating the engineering documentation to support each order configuration. This is a huge difference that saves time and money and dramatically improves order execution. And, if a new product feature or option that is created is made available to other customers, the engineering effort is leveraged across more orders.

Where is the Biggest Opportunity for Mass Customization?

Companies that see profits eroding as product configurability increases are prime candidates for mass customization:

The problem doesn't occur overnight. What once "worked" doesn't anymore—the company hits the wall from an order execution and profitability standpoint. Once you reach this point, your options are to stop offering the

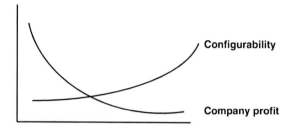

Configurability

Company profit

incremental features and options that contributed to eroding your profits or to find a way to create efficiencies where they don't presently exist. The former option is usually impractical; the latter option is far more desirable as it represents maintaining market share.

Often, companies will find that whenever there is heavy engineering content within individual order configurations that is not a recoverable expense from the customer, mass customization can be an answer. Here are a few industries that come to mind:

- Fire/rescue vehicles
- High technology systems products
- Custom semiconductor chips
- Automotive
- Aircraft
- Construction and building products
- Doors, windows, kitchen cabinets, and enclosures
- Hardware: locks, closures, and mounting devices
- Telecommunication systems
- Hydraulic/pneumatic equipment: fluid power, cylinders, and valves
- Industrial equipment: elevators, hoses, and conveyors
- Industrial process equipment
- Material handling, storage racks, and cranes
- Lighting: industrial, commercial, aircraft, and food
- Heating, ventilation, air conditioning (HVAC), refrigeration, and electrical power equipment

- Vehicles/farm equipment: bus, trailers, recreational vehicles, and trucks
- Boats/yachts

Most companies are focused on making the transition from the engineer-to-order business paradigm to mass customization. Why is this?

- Most mass producers aren't even considering transitioning to mass customization.
- There is a lot of pain associated with producing orders for highly engineered products.

Let's consider the diagram below:

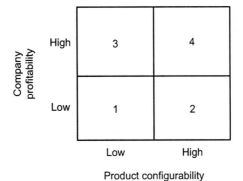

Product configurability

Most manufacturers of configurable products are in a state "2" which is characterized by low profits and a high level of product configurability. The desired state is "4" high profits while maintaining high product configurability. How should you define "high profitability?" Certainly, you want to be equal to or better than the market leader in your industry. Manufacturers considering implementing mass customization want to move from "2" to "4" or "3" to "4."

I'd like you to note that in the diagram above, I use the expression "company profitability." I have intentionally avoided the use of the terms "gross margin," "operating margin," and "profit margin," as those terms can be misleading. At the end of the day, what investors care about is "are

Mass Customization 23

profits levels meeting expectations as a company," not "how are you accounting for your expenses." Most engineer-to-order companies have significant engineering expense that is usually accounted from under "research and development" expense rather than an expense directly associated with producing customer orders. "Gross margin" and "operating margin" do not reflect these engineering expenses and, as a result, there is a distortion. It is for this reason that I advocate "company profitability."

The following white paper illustrates some of the pain points within one industry producing highly configured products:

Wall Street Journal Proclaims "Firetrucks Go High Tech" Yet Processes for Selling, Engineering and Producing Them Lag Fire/Rescue Vehicle Manufacturer Needs

It is wonderful when the *Wall Street Journal* (*WSJ*) recognizes the achievements and progress in the fire/rescue industry. On July 25, 2005, Timothy W. Martin, *WSJ* Staff Reporter, wrote an article titled Fire Trucks Go High Tech and subtitled Spurred by 9/11 Spending, Rigs Cost Up to $1 Million; 29,000 Options, Even A Sink.

The article reviews the complexities of a tiller ladder truck ordered by the North Hudson, New Jersey, fire department and other departments. Mr. Martin did a masterful job depicting how the mission of the fire departments has evolved from firefighting to include rescue, hazmat, and emergency medical services, and how, as a consequence, the configurability of trucks has grown exponentially. Yet, the processes for selling, engineering and producing these vehicles lag industry needs.

Those of us who have been involved in the process of ordering and producing fire/rescue vehicles understand that each order configuration represents a painful and arduous birthing process. It is difficult for departments to decide what features and options they are going to need on a vehicle that will have a useful life of 8–15 years or more. It is even more difficult for vehicle manufacturers in this intensely competitive industry to engineer and produce customized vehicles limited only by the imagination of the committees that specify them and the budgets of the municipalities and agencies that buy them.

The fire/rescue vehicle manufacturers have a "dirty little secret" not revealed in the *WSJ* article—these highly configured vehicles all too often yield little if any profit. This is killing many manufacturers. The challenge these manufacturers face is reducing the extraordinarily high level of engineering content per order configuration. The current challenge brings with it a good number of potential as well as costly problems:

- Late customer deliveries—a lack of smooth order flow through the factory often caused by the discovery of missing parts at critical points during the building process
- Frequent margin disappointments due to underestimating costs that are not clearly understood when the order is accepted
- Engineering effort incurred to support each order configuration:

  - Is non-recoverable expense
  - Typically cannot be leveraged into future orders
  - Overwhelms engineering's ability to create new products and enhance existing products

It would make a lot of sense for fire/rescue vehicle manufacturers to shift from the current "engineer-to-order" paradigm to a "mass customization" paradigm. Under mass customization, the product options are pre-engineered and modularized so the customers and dealers can recompose them into highly customized order configurations specified through electronic selling tools seamlessly connected to the factory. Mass customization allows for 90% or more of the order configuration's engineering effort to be completed in advance of the order taking, ensures cost and margins are understood, and provides the dealer with a significant range of options from which to configure a customer's order. The offerings can go far beyond what has become commonly known as limited option "program trucks."

A business and industry that cannot make money is in a precarious state. Fire/rescue vehicle manufacturers cannot continue to try to be all things to all people if their financial health and viability is continually compromised. There is a better way. As this transformation can't occur overnight, it is best to get started sooner rather than later and advisable to get outside assistance to drive this critical transformational initiative.

Mass production channel distribution strategies (dealers and retailers) actually discourage a customer-driven business paradigm. This isn't to suggest there aren't worthwhile opportunities for mass producers to examine this business model. Manufacturers of mass-produced high-end capital goods, e.g., automobiles, would benefit tremendously from the mass customization business paradigm.

As I write this, the price of gasoline is over $4 per gallon across the United States; prices are more than double this in Europe, Asia, and India. Since the year 2001, the average price of gasoline has risen from $1.45 per gallon to its present levels. While we've seen spikes into the low $3 range, the impact of $4 per gallon gas has automobile manufacturers scratching their heads about how to sell their vast inventories of sports utility vehicles (SUVs) and big trucks. The process of leasing vehicles is about to become extinct—a key financing mechanism to sell automobile inventory. Why? If there is no way to predict the future residual value of a vehicle, the risk of leasing it is too great. Who wants to buy large vehicles now? The market is shrinking. The value of large SUVs and trucks coming off lease is going to only flood the market with vehicles that no one really wants. To dump them will mean one thing: selling them at a loss or scrapping them.

Would mass customization have helped the automobile manufacturers under this scenario? Yes. The automobile manufacturers would not be stuck with the finished goods inventory presently available in the distribution channel. They would only be producing actual orders based on customer demand. Now, they might be caught flat-footed with respect to some key components that they likely purchase based on a forecast: engines and transmissions. But, to put those engines and transmissions into vehicles (finished goods) that no one really wants certainly limits what can be done with them.

Let's consider Dell under a similar scenario. Assume that Intel introduces a microprocessor chip that renders computers built with the previous generation of microprocessor chips undesirable. Once the old microprocessor chips are installed in finished goods inventory, there is no return. But, if Dell only produces the motherboards on demand that contain the old microprocessor chips, it doesn't incur a situation of having finished goods inventory sitting around in inventory hoping that a customer wants it.

If it did, it would likely have to deeply discount the finished goods products to sell the inventory.

Building based on actual customer demand is efficient and ensures that finished goods inventory doesn't become obsolete due to changes in market conditions. This is a key benefit of mass customization: building finished products only after receipt of a firm customer order.

4 Attributes of a Mass Customizer

If you are a discrete manufacturer, what is it like to be a mass customizer? How do you know you've reached that state? Here are the attributes of a mass customizer that matter most:

- Offers custom product configurations derived from standardized product modules or product modularity (or components or capabilities). This, of course, assumes that there has been a "product rationalization" effort to identify those essential options that the marketplace will require.

- Maintains a listing—usually within a product configurator—of standardized product modules as well as any rules for combining the product modules into fully configured products.

- Provides a means to seamlessly share the same understanding about product configurability across the enterprise (with customers, distributors, sales, order administration, engineering, manufacturing, and service).

- Extends the capability to create order configurations and explore alternatives to its customers and distributors (extended enterprise) via a product configurator. This product configurator allows customers to conduct a "what if" analysis looking at different product and pricing options. Ideally, the system should identify the lead time to obtain an order configuration. [Note: Three things a customer really cares about are (1) what are my options, (2) how much is this configuration going to cost, and (3) how long will it take to produce it? Truly effective systems need to address all of these issues.]

- Views the likelihood that any two order configurations would be identical as a coincidence.

- Builds configured orders only after receipt of an order—does not stock any finished products. (Note: This is not to imply that there aren't subassemblies and parts sitting on the shelf to support order demand. It means these parts aren't allocated to specific orders until after an order is booked by the manufacturer.)

- Engineering is not involved in the creation of a bill of material to support individual order configurations.

(a) Where should engineering focus its time and energy? Creating documentation to support production?

(b) Day-to-day quote validation and order taking?

(c) Focus on innovation to grow business while unburdening engineering from tedious work?

The correct answer is "c."

- Order demand driven directly to manufacturing via a sales order.

- Engineering involved only when a new product module is needed or to finalize the engineering work on things that must be postponed until just before the order hits the factory. For example, engineering may need to confirm certain items prior to production commencing.

- Engineering defines "allowable" product configurations based on technical feasibility, not marketing or sales policy. This is important. You do not want to change the logic behind allowable or permissible configurations every time the marketing or sales philosophy changes. To do otherwise creates constant rework and churn.

- Engineering designs the product with product modularity in mind.

- Product management makes determinations about "saleable" product configurations.

- No people-dependency for expert knowledge about product configurations.

- A "mass customizer" needs to be a "progressive manufacturer."

Progressive Manufacturers infuse *technology* into all areas of their business to *create sustainable competitive advantage* by *connecting* the *customer* to the *manufacturing* process. (David Brousell, *Managing Automation*, Progressive Manufacturing Summit 2006: 7 Rules to Win in a Global Market; emphasis added)

This is an incredibly important concept in terms of implementing mass customization. Each highlighted word embodies the essence of mass customization.

Can a company be a mass customizer and meet only a few of the attributes enumerated above? No. They are all critical.

These attributes demonstrate why mass customization is really an enterprise-wide business opportunity, not a departmental challenge. We're going to look at why this is the case in Chapter 5 in greater detail.

Mass Customization Implementation: What's Different?

Under mass customization, engineering no longer provides top assembly bills of material to describe each customer order configuration. The top assembly bill is replaced by the ERP sales order and work order. Engineering's role shifts to working with product management to define the modules and manage the configuration rules that govern how the modules can ultimately be combined into saleable order configurations.

In a mass customization environment, product management and engineering are responsible for

1. Defining and releasing the modules (basic product building blocks, features, and options) that will be used in producing customer orders
2. Defining the mapping between the sales view of the building blocks (models, features, and options) and the manufacturing view (parts and assemblies)
3. Defining the technical feasibility and expert knowledge for combining modules into actual configurations
4. Supporting the integration and release of new features and options into the product line

These are much higher value-added activities than creating and maintaining bills of material to support order configurations. If engineering is no longer creating top assembly bills of material, how do they communicate allowable configuration information with the rest of the enterprise?

Engineering and product management need a means to capture the expert knowledge concerning the configurability of products. Such functionality or capability is generally not available as part of ERP through any means other than a bill of material. For simple products or in situations where it is not cost-effective to generate a sophisticated information technology application, a paper-based configuration guide may suffice. Otherwise, a software application will be needed to capture and manage the expert knowledge about products.

Leveraging Configuration Knowledge across the Enterprise

The expert configuration knowledge can be shared across the enterprise to support functions such as

- Providing a means for a customer, dealer, reseller, or sales to properly configure a customer's order.

- Providing a means for marketing to restrict the set of choices available to a customer even if the choices are technically feasible from an engineering point of view.

- Validating a customer's order requirements.

- Conducting a "what-if" configuration analysis to determine product costs and lead times based on the presence or absence of certain features and options.

- Quoting.

- Forecasting.

- Mapping the customer's order requirements to the parts needed to actually manufacture the product. For example, if someone configures a truck, they would need to specify an engine and a transmission. The interface kit that mates the engine with the transmission would need to be added to the order even though the kit is likely not an attribute that the customer would specify on the order.

- Determining the parts the factory actually needs to manufacture the customer's order based on plant-specific and/or engineering-specific product changes that are in the queue.
- Staging products under development for future release.

The Role of ERP in Mass Customization

In a mass customization environment, ERP accommodates all traditional manufacturing company functional needs: parts item master; bills of material; supply chain functions such as inventory control, material requirements planning, purchasing, and production control; sales orders; and accounting.

However, other than bills of material, ERP does not provide any means for engineering to define configurable products. Engineering needs to have a mechanism that is outside of ERP but can be easily integrated with ERP to accommodate this need. And, why does engineering need this tool? Engineering is the only organization that has the expert knowledge about parts and sub-assemblies required to support this mission-critical business need.

What about Sales Configurators?

As we've discussed, mass customization is an enterprise-wide business strategy, not a "front-office" or departmental problem. Effective mass customization implementations will favorably affect customers, sales, marketing, order administration, engineering, manufacturing, service, and finance. Sales configurators are generally "front-office" tools that do little more than automate the price list.

In general, sales configurators are not integrated with the "back office" and therein lies the key problem. Customer order requirements must be interpreted by order administration, engineering, and/or manufacturing. This introduces errors and operational difficulties that adversely affect customer satisfaction. The customer's order is seldom (if ever) in alignment with the bills of material and the expert product knowledge. A sales configurator can actually be a step backward as senior management incorrectly believes that it solves an enterprise-wide problem when quite the opposite is true.

Attributes of a Mass Customizer

5 Back to Basics: Quote-to-Cash

I like to keep things simple. The basic flow with in a company is to design a product or feature followed by

- Quoting
- Ordering (customer purchase order)
- Book (enter the order into the ERP system)
- Build (open work orders, kit, build, test, and inspect)
- Ship
- Install/deliver
- Cash collection
- Service/support

Quote to cash

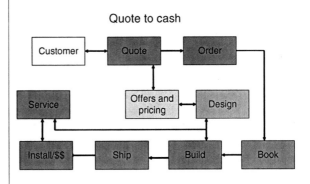

The flowchart above starts (as all mass customization discussions should) with the customer. The customer is the driver of order demand under a mass customization business paradigm. In articles I have written, I have used the expression "customer-driven manufacturing." That's what mass customization is all about: the customer drives the order configuration based on what's been defined as "allowable options." The "allowable options" are essentially a "buffet table" from which the customer selects how they want their order configuration to look. The process of determining what the allowable options are is called "product rationalization."

The ultimate goal of the customer is getting a quote that identifies what they are going to get, how much it is going to cost them, and how long it will take to receive the order. It is perfectly reasonable to quote an expected lead time after receipt of order and to make the customer aware that the order lead time can only be confirmed after order receipt. Circumstances change all the time affecting lead times. There is usually a delay between the time a quote is generated and an order placed so this shouldn't be an unreasonable burden for both parties in the transaction to accept.

In order to be able to get a quote, the product configurator needs to be populated with what I refer to as "offers and pricing"—what is being offered and at what price? We described that above as "product rationalization."

To be able to establish pricing, it is necessary to have a good estimate of (1) what item(s) is/are needed to satisfy the option requirements, (2) the standard cost of the components (material cost, labor, and burden) needed to satisfy the option requirements, and (3) the lead time to procure the items needed to satisfy the option requirement. Thus, to do this properly, there needs to be "linkage" between the design bill of material and the labor routings, to effectively put the option in the selling tool with an appropriate selling price and lead time. Most companies do not have an effective process for doing this.

Too often, companies use crude estimates with respect to establishing pricing for options, both standard options and new requests for options that don't yet exist. This is problematic as it often yields order configuration margin surprises—usually negative margin surprises. A company needs to have an effective process for creating new features and options consistent with the demands of the business. It is only reasonable to expect that, despite the best efforts to rationalize products, there will always be new features and options needed to satisfy customers. The process for adding features and options needs to be responsive to the customer's needs. I liken this process to something akin to an air traffic control system. There will always be new options arriving and old options departing. A company must have a process for seamlessly managing those transitions.

Once the quotation is acceptable, the customer (or his representative) can place an order. The order is "booked" once it is confirmed as being acceptable to the company. It is at this "booking" point in the process that an order confirmation is sent to the customer confirming all details associated with the order. Many companies create a "sales order" in their ERP system to "book the order."

When the booked order hits the factory for processing, a work order is generally opened to initiate the processes of building the order. This work order enables materials to be issued and labor to be accrued against the customer order, order production to occur, testing, and final quality control.

Shipping, installing, and collecting money are no different than any other manufacturing company. It should be noted that one of the more problematic areas with highly configured products is getting paid due to discrepancies perceived by the customer between "what they ordered" and "what they received." This happens most often when there is a great deal of engineering effort required after the order is booked that results in interpretations being made for what engineering thinks the customer is really asking for.

The last area—support—can be very problematic for highly configured products if there isn't good discipline in the factory for producing the products, part, and subassemblies. There is also the issue of having the appropriate complement of spare parts needed to support customers consistent with their expectations. Products evolve over time. The "latest" part won't always work in every situation. The handcrafting of parts creates problems when those parts are subsequently damaged or fail and need to be replaced in the field. This is particularly true if things are built according to "tribal knowledge" or hand-fitted.

Each of the following areas represents a customer touch-point or experience point dealing with your company:

- Quoting
- Ordering (customer purchase order)
- Book (enter the order into the ERP system)
- Build (open work orders, kit, build, test, and inspect)
- Ship
- Install/deliver
- Cash collection
- Service/support

Each bullet point above represents a point where your company can favorably predispose companies to do business with you now and in the future. It is the sum of customer experiences dealing with your company that determines whether or not you'll get an opportunity to work with them again.

Implementing mass customization must be approached holistically due to all the interdependencies between the customer and the organizations that must support the customer. Sadly, companies with configurable products often don't approach this challenge holistically. A holistic approach yields the best operational flow and efficiency. Your company's processes must be designed with mass customization in mind.

6 Implementing Mass Customization

Here's what a typical project involves:

1. Implementing mass customization requires an assessment to understand the business challenges and information needs of dealers, sales, order administration, engineering, materials, manufacturing, and service as well as those who will maintain/support the system. Key issues that arise include the following:

   a. How do customers, dealers, and the sales force think about the product and its configurability; what's working; and what's not?

   b. Quotations—what do they need to look like and how is pricing handled?

   c. Sales orders—how to translate quotations into sales orders within ERP?

   d. Work orders—how to translate sales orders into work orders?

   e. What's the business process for requesting new features and options, getting each request approved and engineered, obtaining cost information and establishing pricing, and updating the configurator with the new feature or option?

Let's review each of these bullet points in greater detail.

When you ask people for their opinion, get ready to learn something important. If you are reading this book, it is because you are all too familiar with the pain experienced by those located externally from headquarters trying to drive orders through your company. The pain experienced at headquarters is greatly magnified in the field. Try to gain an understanding from a broad range of dealers and customers, not just the top tier.

In terms of quotations, will you simply need a list of features and options with prices or more detailed specifications associated with each feature and option? Will you want to provide line item pricing or a bundled price for the entire configuration? What will your dealers or customers require?

Migrating a quotation into the ERP order entry module has never proven to be a daunting challenge from a technology point of view. ERP systems typically have an application programming interface that, with some setup, allows for bringing data in from other applications such as a configurator. Yet, it is important that this process be automated to promote greater efficiency and to reduce order entry errors.

Some companies will find that the process of creating a work order (or factory order) from a sales order requires additional parts be added that aren't accounted for on the sales order. This isn't the least bit abnormal. If this is the case, there will need to be a business process to accommodate this need.

In terms of a process for new features and options, it is critical that a company have a business process that is rigorously followed in all situations. Don't compromise your process due to urgent or emergency circumstances—simply drive the process faster. It is the "exceptions" that cause the greatest breakdowns and a new feature or option shouldn't compromise a company's essential control mechanisms "for the sake of expediency." If a customer needs something that isn't available, the same process used to rationalize and add other features and options should be followed. Not only should this process consider design and manufacturing issues, but also costing and pricing. These are details that need to be worked out before an order is accepted, not after. This is critical!

2. Mass customization implementation often involves transitioning the enterprise away from an "engineer-to-order" or a "mass production" paradigm—it is essential that you create a shared vision of how business will be different with the introduction of a configurator.

How will the business be different? It is imperative that expectations be set and followed, particularly with respect to the items raised in point 1 above.

For example, under an "engineer-to-order" business paradigm, a company may have been willing to do just about anything and everything that has been requested by a customer or dealer, irrespective of whether it made business sense to do so. Under a mass customization paradigm, that likely won't be the case. Some will see this as a threat to their livelihoods; others will take the decision in their stride. You want to do something for a customer because it creates a win–win situation in that moment, not win–lose. Some folks will dangle future business opportunities as hinging on the one situation you face today. Sometimes it will be valid and true; sometimes it will be a ploy. If you take on too many "win–lose" propositions, the manufacturer ends up losing in the short-term/near-term and perhaps in the long-term. Someone has to make the tough calls. That is the role of product management.

3. Configurator implementation often requires a "make" or "buy" decision with respect to the configurator technology needs. This decision should not be the first step in implementing mass customization. Selecting the wrong technology can thwart a project's success. See Chapter 7 for more on this subject.

4. There must be a product rationalization process—deciding "what" and "what not" to offer the marketplace.

Deciding "what" and "what not" to offer will be the subject of endless debate. Dealers and customers tend to only care about what they want and say "to heck" with everyone else. It is not easy striking a balance in terms of what to offer yet the balance needs to be struck during this process. Your offerings must have sufficient breadth to be relevant to customers which means if you can't give them exactly what they want, you offer them a viable alternative.

For example, when I worked on a mass customization project with a fire/rescue vehicle manufacturer, we decided to standardize the front and rear truck compartment widths rather than allowing customers to specify whatever width they wanted within a range. So, if a customer requested a 26.5-inch wide front compartment, the dealer would work with the customer to determine if they would accept a 28-inch wide front compartment. Without exception, we found that the 28-inch wide compartment was a suitable alternative. Customers will often accept what you offer them in terms of choice if they simply are presented with the realities of what you are offering. Otherwise, customers think they start with a blank sheet of paper and specify what they want.

We found other situations where the same customer was not willing to compromise: e.g., the warning light bar on the top of the cab on the fire truck. While on low-end program trucks, we had the ability to limit the selection; on the higher-end custom trucks, the customer simply wanted what they wanted and we came to understand that we needed to be able to accommodate their requests. This was simply a cost of doing business.

5. The bill of material structure must be modularized and aligned with the features and options that are deemed necessary.

It is the alignment of the features and options with the bill of material structure that creates great efficiencies and can eliminate translation errors. If there isn't complete alignment, then it is necessary for engineering to create documentation to support the ordering of parts as well as production documentation for each and every order. Inadvertent omissions within bills of materials create significant, negative downstream implications and create the need for last-minute engineering changes.

If you want to have a continuous flow from order receipt through manufacturing, focus on getting the bill of material and documentation for each feature and option correct up front.

6. It is necessary to determine the rules for allowable configurations meaning identifying what features and options can coexist with other features and options in the same final configuration. It is also necessary to determine what configuration interdependencies exist.

One of the key roles of a product configurator is setting expectations about "what works with what" and preventing configurations from being created that cannot possibly be built. For example, if certain transmissions can only be used with certain engines, it is imperative that the configurator system allow for transmission choices that are allowed based on the engine selection.

7. Developing a process and tools to create the data needed for the configurator system and subsequently added to the configurator: Depending on the magnitude of your project, you will be creating a lot of information or repackaging existing information into an entirely new form. There will be lot of data that needs to be created and managed to support this configurator development effort. You must give careful thought to how you create and maintain this information. In some cases, you'll need to develop tools in simple spreadsheets or perhaps even new, custom applications to support the creation and maintenance of the data required to support the configurator. It's important to remember that the effort never stops—you'll forever be creating, adding, and integrating new features and options, so it's important to thoughtfully create the infrastructure required to support this ongoing activity.

You'll need a process that allows you to stage new features and options before distributing them to a broader audience once the new feature or option is released.

You may want technology and a business process that allows for staging pricing updates to become effective on certain dates as well as a way to stage features and options to appear or disappear on certain dates. You may also want to be able to note that certain features won't be available for shipment until a specific time frame or date or that certain features won't be available for new orders after a certain date.

8. Developing a means to electronically disseminate updates to the configurator system: Unless you have a Web-enabled application, users of your configurator application will need to have information updated locally on their computer systems. You need a technology and process for doing this. What kinds of updates will there be? New features and options, specification changes, pricing changes, and new products will be commonplace.

Wouldn't it make sense to only have a Web-based configurator application? The answer again is "it depends." Having a Web-based configurator application requires that a user be tethered to the Internet in order to access the information. With all the technology that is available today, the notion of being tethered to headquarters has become much less of a problem than it was even recently when dial-up Internet connections were the only option. However, if you are configuring oil-drilling equipment in a remote area of the world without a cell phone tower nearby, you may find that you need a configurator application that can run as a stand-alone without any connection. This is a usability characteristic that you need to understand. Some organizations will want the flexibility to have the capability of working either tethered to the Internet or in a non-tethered mode. If your business requirement is to support both modes, this certainly adds another layer of complexity and cost to your implementation.

9. In situations where profitability is at issue, a project may include implementing activity-based costing so senior management can truly understand the profitability of individual products and product lines. (There is more about this subject in Chapter 8.)

Activity-based costing likely won't be adopted as a replacement for traditional cost accounting as is reflected in most ERP systems. It will, however, provide much greater insight into actual costs as it takes indirect costs and considers them as direct costs. And, you may find over time that company moves away from standard costing due to the distortions that it can create.

10. Testing order configurations through the process: To the extent possible, you'll want to compare "identical" configurations created in both the old/new systems to see what differences arise so they can be reconciled. The finance and accounting folks will be very nervous about the transition to a new product structure and resulting changes to cost associated with those changes.

11. Educating the organization how to do business differently in this new, mass customization business paradigm: Every company has a "this is how we do it here" mentality, an inertia that is challenging to divert to a new path. It is not enough to merely announce change. The team leading the project must evangelize the project as well as the coming change and ensure that people understand what is happening and why it is happening. You need to set expectations and ensure that those expectations are met.

12. Examining the corporate data model and looking for interface requirements: Your shiny new configurator system does not exist in a vacuum—it exists within existing infrastructure. It may pull information from one system and populate it in your system. All these interfaces need to be clearly understood as well as the method for refreshing the data in the configurator system and other business systems.

13. A full roll-out is necessary to all users of the new system—What is needed to make each category of user successful? Whenever there is change in an organization, it creates tension. Most projects underestimate the training needs and organizational adoption issues that will arise during the transition from old to new systems. Why?

Projects are generally late, over budget, and management wants to get to the finish line quickly.

It is critical to understand that you are doing this for the users of the new tool and processes, not for yourself. It is not unusual for there to be resistance, but it is very important that you address the issues that arise in other than a dismissive manner. However much time you allow for training and adoption will never be sufficient. Be generous in allocating adequate time to make the transition to the new tools and processes.

7 Product Configurators for Mass Customization

Implementing mass customization requires a product configurator. Product configurators are software applications that enable customers to order exactly what they need based on allowable choices.

A product configurator that is accessible or viewable by a customer (either directly or through their sales representative) is key to becoming customer-driven. Thus, the tool needs to be appropriate (usable) by your sales representatives and/or customers. The user interface for most ERP-related functionality is inappropriate for a customer or their representative to consider using.

Customers want to understand what is possible, understand the implications of certain choices and pricing, and hopefully understand the lead time associated with getting the total solution based on order configuration choices that they make.

The product configurator allows customers to buy what they want within allowable limits without requiring that engineering bear the burden of creating and maintaining separate bills of material for each discrete configuration selected by a customer. Increased efficiencies in sales, marketing, engineering, and manufacturing and greater customer satisfaction enable companies to realize the untapped potential of true mass customization.

I liken a product configurator to a menu, much like a menu in a restaurant. Items that fall within the menu can be ordered without restriction. Items that aren't on the menu must be approved and added to the menu before the customized item (configuration) can be priced, quoted, and ordered.

A product configurator helps a person quickly converge on a valid configuration within the product line's capabilities, to precisely summarize the customization, and to be the source of information transmitted to your order entry system and subsequently to the factory. Product configurators also support the evolution of a product line's capabilities over time. An optional, but impressive, capability is the display of what the configured product looks like using advanced graphics capabilities. They can also be used to quickly and easily prepare quotations and drive forecasting.

Product configurators achieve their greatest value when deployed for use by your customers. For this reason, more and more configurator applications are deployed via the Internet or extranets (secure Internet-accessible Web sites). If you are reluctant to expose your customers to such a tool, I encourage you to, at a minimum, place the configurator application in the hands of your sales force.

When companies implement a product configurator for headquarters' use only, but not the field staff, the configuration process is left to the imagination of their sales team and customers. They run the risk of disappointing customers when you have to inform them that you cannot provide products that you have already quoted or, worse, have been accepted as orders.

Configurator Development and Implementation

A product configurator can either be developed from scratch or purchased as a stand-alone application enabler tool kit that you customize to reflect your needs.

While the future trend may be to purchase a configurator application enabler tool kit that can be integrated with customer relationship management (CRM) business software and MRP/ERP applications, I am very leery of "configurators" sold as part of MRP/ERP systems as most rely on pre-packaged configurations, an approach that is inconsistent with mass customization. Also, the MRP/ERP user interface is usually unacceptable for sales and customer interaction.

It is critically important that you develop or acquire the appropriate configurator technology based on your company's needs. Not all configurator technologies are the same. There are essentially three types of product configurators:

1. Features and options
2. Parameter-driven
3. A hybrid of "feature and option" and "parameter-driven"

Before selecting a configurator, you should carefully define your current and predicted needs. Then, make sure you are getting the appropriate configurator technology for your needs.

The product configurator can also be looked at as an "air traffic control system" in that it sets expectations about what is available, what is being discontinued, and what is being added over time. For example, a manufacturer may decide that an option is not available after a certain date due to product transitions, changes in regulatory, e.g., Environmental Protection Agency (EPA) and requirements. Pricing changes often occur for the same item purchased at a certain point in time; this needs to be accounted for and, if possible, staged in the system.

New features need to be staged in the product configurator so they can be ordered even though they may not ship before a certain date. A really effective system allows this to happen.

It is a mistake to view a configurator as a tool just for sales. A configurator gives you the opportunity to achieve greater efficiencies in sales, engineering, and manufacturing. Making the transition to mass customization can (and should) be a company-wide initiative. Many companies limit the scope of their configurator effort to "automating the price list" and never realize the benefits.

Here are some critical questions:

- Can an "off-the-shelf" package satisfy your organizations unique needs?

- What happens if your competitor decides to implement the same "off-the-shelf" system?

- If you buy an "off-the-shelf" application, what customization or personalization is required? What integration is required with other applications?

- If you decide it is best to "make" the configurator software, it is necessary to develop the requirements, develop the software, the test and integration plan, etc.

- Are you concerned about seizing competitive advantage and truly distinguishing yourself in your marketplace? If so, a customized system may be your best choice.

Selecting the appropriate configurator technology can make or break a project. There are approximately 100 different companies offering configurator technologies today. The business is very competitive and there aren't an exorbitant number of opportunities for companies to sell their technology and implementation services.

Can an off-the-shelf configurator package satisfy your organization's unique needs? This is difficult to answer as the answer usually is "it depends"—it depends on what you need; whether or not the solution is scalable, easily supportable, and maintainable; and whether it has a user interface that infrequent users to the application can become acquainted with.

Configurator companies often use very simple examples to demonstrate their technology's capabilities and you find that the solution does not easily allow for the addition of new features and options nor does it scale well to the most complex products that you currently offer. Don't start with your simplest product, determine that it works just fine and assume that you'll be able to make it work with your most complex products. You want to find out early on "if you can get there from here." Start with your most complex offerings and convince yourself that the solution will scale effectively for you.

What happens if you and your competitor implement the same configurator technology? While you could be concerned about differentiation, there may also be a concern about whether both companies have made an absolutely brilliant choice by selecting the same configurator or both have made the same colossal mistake. It is not unheard of for two companies in same industry to make the same mistake selecting inappropriate configurator technology..

Implementing a configurator isn't about reaching a destination, it's about supporting a journey—the journey of today's products as well as tomorrow's products, products that you may know little or nothing about when you make the decision to go with a vendor's technology.

Implementing a configurator is about customization and personalization; whether the issue be about system outputs, e.g., quotations and specifications, or about how you chose to rationalize and present your features and options. If you work with dealers, dealers will want system outputs to embody their branding as well as yours.

Another common issue about using an "off-the-shelf" configurator is that it could be harder to distinguish yourself in your marketplace. That is why some companies favor developing a proprietary solution from scratch.

If you chose to "make" (rather than buy) configurator technology, then you need to understand that you will be in the software development and software maintenance business (even if you outsource the technology development and maintenance) but you are likely to have a solution that is very well adapted to your business. Is custom software more expensive? It may be and it may not be. Depending on the extent of the customizations required on the "off-the-shelf" package, it could be a wash or even less expensive. There is no simple answer to this question.

The configurator technology is but one part of the overall solution. It is a critically important piece of a successful implementation but the best software in the world needs a plan to make it coherent and relevant.

8 Key Enablers and Mistakes Implementing Mass Customization

The key enablers of mass customization are

- Enterprise-wide organizational adoption
- Institutionalizing a product management function
- Deciding what to offer the marketplace—product rationalization
- Appropriate product configurator technology
- Recognition that mass customization is a paradigm shift
- Activity-based costing

Enterprise-wide Organizational Adoption

If you want to seamlessly connect your customers to the enterprise, it is essential that you approach implementation across the entire enterprise and the extended enterprise, the latter being customers and/or dealers. As has been said earlier, mass customization is about being customer-driven. You have to structure your business from this mindset. Failure to approach mass customization as an enterprise-wide initiative is to keep many of the pain points we've discussed earlier:

- Having great disruptions in order fulfillment flow from order administration through the factory
- Incorrectly setting expectations about what is permissible
- Booking orders that can't be manufactured

Institutionalizing a Product Management Function

Sales' role is taking orders; marketing's role is creating interest and desire for products. Product management has a much more holistic role and responsibility to the enterprise. Product management needs to be responsible for determining specifically what to offer the marketplace and ensuring that the product works from a financial point of view. Product management is like the chef in the restaurant—determining what goes on the menu and the pricing for the item. Product management has to drive the evolution of the product line; nothing stays in a steady state and succeeds. As market tastes change, so must the product offerings. Product management needs to be that calm, rational entity that impartially helps the company launch new products, features, and options in a seamless fashion and advises senior management of the organizational readiness for launching new products, features, and options.

Included within product management's charter is helping the enterprise assess and understand the impact of a new product on demand for existing products and product lines. This includes ensuring that demand for current products doesn't fall off a cliff before the ramp-up of the new product occurs. Product management helps the enterprise manage the inventory transition to minimize excess and obsolete inventory.

There are product development business processes that can be implemented that include a comprehensive examination of appropriateness of the product and/or feature from conception through launch. They do much more than simply manage the development of a new product— they incorporate essential review of the market and business issues throughout the product development process up to and including product launch.

Deciding What to Offer the Marketplace: Product Rationalization

A company has to decide precisely what it is willing to offer the marketplace in terms of product configurability. If this is left to the imagination of the customer and/or the dealer, chaos ensues. There needs to be enough differentiation between different features and options that it makes business sense to offer it without. It is often best to offer a feature or option because you must to make the offering relevant to the marketplace, not merely because you can. Since no company has an infinite amount of engineering resources to design different features and options, careful decisions must be made about what needs to be offered. Will your offerings be sufficient or are you likely to find customers who want something different? Let me offer you another restaurant analogy.

The waitress at your favorite Mexican restaurant asks if you'd like an appetizer. You pause and tell her you feel like having escargot. She informs you they don't have escargot. You tell her that it's really important to her and you'd like her to speak to the chef about preparing this for you.

She heads to the kitchen and announces to the chef that "there's some nut in the dining room who has his heart set on having some escargot for an appetizer." There are three questions that the chef has to ponder:

1. Can they do it?
2. Do they want to do it?
3. If so, at what price and lead time can they do it?

The chef may decide:

- No way—decline the customer's request.
- "Why not" and contact a French restaurant three doors away to get some escargot for the customer charging the customer what the French restaurant would charge him.
- Yes, it will take 3 hours to prepare the escargot at a price of $100.

The chef should also consider if this is the beginning of an exciting new trend—customers may want escargot in his Mexican restaurant and, as a result, he should take the appropriate steps to add this to his regular menu.

Interestingly enough, this restaurant metaphor mirrors what happens with manufactured products. The preceding illustration gives you a sense of the decision matrix a company should use in trying to assess whether or not provide the "special" feature or option the customer is requesting. Again, the questions that need to be asked and answered are

• Can we do it?

• Do we want to do it?

• If so, at what price and lead time can we do it?

• Do we do this for one customer or it is likely others will want it so you "add it to the menu?"

• If we don't do it, what is the likelihood the entire order will be lost?

The following diagram helps a company decide whether or not there is value in offering a new feature or option or even a new product based on the expected return when contrasted with the cost and effort of producing that return:

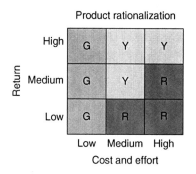

Product rationalization

Green (G) = good "yes" probability
Yellow (Y) = 50/50 "yes" probability
Red (R) = very low "yes" probability

Obviously, the best situation for the manufacturer is the "high return/low effort" projects whereas the worst situation is the "high effort/low return" projects. The "specials" in the green area are the specials you will likely do whereas those in red are the ones that should be declined. "Specials" in the yellow area need to have sales potential beyond the current order demand.

"George Kluge Truck"

This is a true story; only the salesman's name has been changed. A fire/rescue vehicle manufacturer had an infamous salesman working for a particular dealer named George Kluge. George did everything he could to preclude competitors from bidding on trucks that he wanted to sell. How did he do this?

George carried around binders containing pictures of every crazy feature and option ever devised on fire trucks. He helped his customers understand that there were profound advantages to building trucks that contained many of these crazy features. He convinced his customers they needed "the biggest, baddest fire trucks in the industry."

For example, if a normal truck had a 3-foot wide bumper extension on the front of the truck, why not put a 4- or 5-foot deep bumper extension on the front of the truck? After all, consider how many more tools you can put in that bumper or how much more fire hose you could carry there.

Well, when you string together a specification for a fire truck that contains so many crazy features, George discovered that none of his competitors were willing to bid on the same truck. (His competitors were smart!)

You would have to question the sanity of the manufacturer who accepted George Kluge's orders. Not only were these trucks a nightmare to engineer, they were a nightmare to manufacture and an even bigger nightmare to support. The orders were always delivered quite late to customer expectations. The warranty costs for George's trucks represented a significant percentage of the total corporate warranty cost compared with other dealers and territories. And, the customers were frustrated that their one-of-a-kind trucks were often unavailable for service due to technical and warranty issues.

The company complained vehemently about George's trucks yet they never turned down his orders.

What is the moral of the story?

The last person in the world you want doing the product rationalization is a salesman who has no skin in the game when it comes to the
ultimate margin on a truck or the warranty expense side. George's
commission was based on the sales price of the truck!

Appropriate Product Configurator Technology

You'll notice I mention "appropriate product configurator technology." Why
"appropriate?" All too often, companies select technology that is not well
matched for their business and end up scrapping the project. If you select
the wrong technology, it is very easy to paint yourself into a corner in such
a way that compromises the business outcome.

Part of the "appropriateness" is the ease of maintenance—adding new
products, new features and options, correcting errors, changing pricing,
and staging pricing changes. Some aspects of this business need can be
accommodated via the product configurator technology; some have to
be accommodated through a business process (see Chapter 8 for more
information).

Activity-Based Costing

One of the biggest challenges is understanding cost. Standard costing
systems are not terribly effective measures of actual cost in terms of mea-
suring profitability of products and product lines. They tend to allocate
costs in a disproportionate way, particularly if there are vast differences
between products. For example, fire/rescue vehicles come in all shapes,
sizes, and prices, and have dramatically different levels of complexity in
terms of engineering effort and manufacturing material costs and labor
input. Yet, standard costing systems spread overhead as though everything were equal, usually based on cost. Also, all the engineering effort
required to develop the production documentation needed to support the
specific order configuration is seldom accounted for in the cost of sales—it
is considered an engineering expense that is kept off the books.

Activity-based costing provides a means to truly understand cost and profitability that standard costing does not. As Doug Hicks, a consultant I've collaborated with often says about understanding cost, "It is better to be approximately right than precisely wrong."

The "cost of variety" is an important concept with respect to highly configurable products. With highly configurable products, the "cost of variety" is significant and often makes the difference between a profitable or unprofitable business. The "cost of variety" becomes a bigger factor when there are dramatic differences between customizable platforms.

The cost of variety includes additional engineering resources, facilities, and capital equipment of manufacturing or testing related to the manufacturing of a specific product. There is little question that variety adds cost. The real issue becomes the incremental cost of supporting all the variety within the product offerings. There can also be incremental cost of variety associated with unique features and options associated with unique product lines.

For example, when Boeing discontinues the manufacturing of a certain aircraft, e.g., the Boeing 717, this frees a lot of resources from engineering, manufacturing, facilities, and capital equipment. There is a "cost of variety" associated with offering and producing that unique aircraft. This is true for all incremental increases in product offerings.

Activity-based costing can help a company get a better understanding of the cost of variety.

Recognition that Mass Customization Is a Paradigm Shift

A manufacturer's world changes dramatically when shifting to mass customization from either the mass production or engineer-to-order business paradigm. Becoming "customer-driven" and modularizing the product lines represent significant change.

If a manufacturer only approaches mass customization as a departmental issue and does not view the issue holistically across the enterprise, the company undermines the very efficiencies it seeks.

Common Mistakes Implementing Mass Customization

- The first mistake is not approaching mass customization as an enterprise-wide business strategy. Often, this occurs when the product configurator is a "back-office" tool used in order administration to configure orders. The other key mistake in this area is using the product configurator as a departmental solution isolated in a silo separate from the other enterprise functions. Would it be a surprise to see that the headquarters' operations team can't connect the dots between the customer and those who have to manufacture the order configuration?

- The second big mistake is selecting inappropriate product configurator technology. A tool used in one company does not ensure that it will work in your company. Companies and teams are hesitant to acknowledge "we made a mistake" selecting a specific application so they spend months or years trying to "work around the problem." If you need a screwdriver and all you have is a hammer, you can't unscrew a screw. The same is true if you select the wrong product configurator technology. There are in excess of 100 configurator companies all looking to make an impact on the world. Buyers should exercise great caution selecting a tool. A product configurator has not achieved "commodity status" like ERP or CRM—there are lots of opportunities to pick the wrong tool.

- Not having a product management function is another key mistake. Product management is not sales and it is not marketing. This function needs to be seen as being distinctly different from sales and marketing.

- Resource contention is always an issue. Some of the experts within the organization who know about viable configurations will be among the busiest folks in the company. Everyone will want access to them. It is important to create the headroom to let these folks do some very detailed and time-consuming work. It is best to augment resources to assist these folks with the product rationalization work.

- In the world of engineer-to-order and mass customization, a company will suffer severe pain if it tries to be all things to all people. Tough choices need to made that won't win the prize for congeniality. For example, if you were to approach Boeing about putting a fifth engine on a 747, they would tell you it's not possible. Yet, some customer requests are just about as ludicrous. And, as we saw in the "George Kluge Truck" example, some companies will try to do it anyway. Mass customization is not about being limitless in terms of offerings, but about putting reasonable bounds around what you are willing to offer customers.

- It is critical that an organization institutionalize mass customization and the product management function. You can't straddle the fence and be successful. Everyone across the enterprise needs to be aligned with the mass customization mission and vision for this to work really well.

- The last mistake is not seeking outside guidance and assistance in executing a transition from someone who has "been there, done that." The outside assistance isn't about assistance merely implementing a product configurator, but about realigning the people and processes.

Key Enablers and Mistakes Implementing Mass Customization

9 What Manufacturing Executives Want

Manufacturing executives want the following outcomes from their businesses:

- Increased market share
- Delighted customers
- Improved quality
- Improved operating margins
- Differentiation/competitive advantage
- Better business execution
- Lean the business—eliminate waste
- Increased velocity
- Happy employees

Let's examine each of these items within the context of highly customized products.

Increased Market Share

Market share is a measure of how well a company stacks up in comparison with its competitors for the same customers. It doesn't matter whether an industry is growing, shrinking, or flat. It doesn't matter if the market share is measured in terms of unit sales or gross revenues.

For example, we know that Toyota has been gaining market share against U.S. automotive manufacturers for years. We interpret this as saying that Toyota is doing what the marketplace wants whereas the U.S. manufacturers are losing favor with the buying public.

Why is market share important for highly customized products? If you are offering customers what they want (rather than asking them to "settle" for whatever you produce), this can have a positive impact on market share assuming, of course, the pricing is in the same ball park as competitors' offerings. And, there is a further underlying assumption that even with the highly customizable offerings, the company is able to generate sufficient operating margins that make the business viable.

Delighted Customers

It's not simply a matter of whether a customer buys your product today—the larger issue is will they come back the next time they need to make a similar purchase. Part of the decision for repeat business is predicated on the customer's experience as a result of the business they have given you. B. Joseph Pine II and James H. Gilmore discuss the importance of delighted customers in their book *The Experience Economy*. Pine and Gilmore discuss the importance of the total customer experience in terms of impacting the customer's next buying decision. A customer who has to "settle" for something other than what they really wanted has to live with the consequences for months or years to come. A customer who has a less than satisfactory experience will feel less obligated to give the same manufacturer his/her business the next time a buying opportunity arises.

Why are "delighted customers" important for highly customized products? A customer who gets what they want from an order configuration standpoint and receives it in the time frame the company committed—commonly known as "on-time delivery"—is likely to be a repeat customer. One of the key customer frustrations for highly customized products is on-time delivery. Getting them what they want is only part of the operational challenge; meeting their delivery needs is just as important.

Improved Quality

It is difficult to produce a quality product if what you are building is a unit of 1—essentially a prototype. There isn't enough institutional knowledge available for building a single unit. Therefore, quality is often compromised.

Improved Operating Margins

Without predictability, it is difficult to drive operating margin improvements. If the company has little or no experience producing the order configuration, the company often relies on tribal knowledge rather than processes and work instructions. Mistakes lead to unplanned rework which further adds to labor hours. While labor may have been factored into the price quotation, the guesstimate is often wrong. There are no labor standards and, sadly, this is often the explanation for why it takes longer to get orders built. Operating margins suffer for the same reasons quality suffers—manufacturing never gets really good at manufacturing what the customers require.

Differentiation/Competitive Advantage

Why should a customer buy from one manufacturer over another? What distinguishes a company in the marketplace from all the other manufacturers with similar offerings? There are, of course, many ways to differentiate a company in the marketplace, but the key differentiation criteria with highly configurable products are

- Ease of doing business with the firm
- Offering what the customer wants in terms of configuration choices
- Delivery: lead time advantage or, at least, the ability to deliver on time
- Competitive pricing
- Ability to support the customer's product when a problem arises

Lean the Business: Eliminate Waste

Anytime a manufacturer can eliminate waste, you've eliminated time and non-valued-added cost. This only augments a company's ability to create profits from operations, eliminate unnecessary rework, and drive better margins. This also increases the velocity of getting orders through the factory which again enhances a company's ability to compete in its marketplace.

Happy Employees

If a company is not set up to properly accommodate highly configurable products, the result is frustration and poor productivity across the company.

One company I worked with had a VP of sales who educated his sales-people to "get the order no matter what and put the pressure on the factory to figure out how to build it." His team did just that. This practice frustrated customers to no end when they later learned that orders the company had accepted could not be built. It also caused a lot of frustration for engineering and operations trying to figure out if there was a way to produce the order so the sales representative wouldn't have to go back to the customer and tell them the order could not be produced.

Another client I worked with hired a very competent director of customer service who, unknowingly, walked into a minefield of angry and upset customers and sales representatives. Order execution to customer expectations was abysmal across the board. After 6 weeks, she left one evening and was never heard from again. She understood her future and concluded it wasn't what she wanted.

If you leave it to the sales team to set expectations about what can and cannot be manufactured, you are putting your relationships with your customers and employees at risk.

Summary

If your company experiences great pain as a consequence of offering configurable products, your company is simply not set up properly. Configurability is at the heart of the problem, a problem that cannot improve without adopting a different mindset and approach to setting up the business.

Mass customization is not an incremental business improvement; it is a paradigm shift that must be adopted across the enterprise. The benefits are profound.

Mass customization gives companies the ability to delight customers, to increase market share through better differentiation, will be a source of competitive advantage, improves profitability and business execution, increases velocity across the entire enterprise, and creates an environment where employees feel like they can succeed when they come to work each day.

If you find your company is suffering as a result of product configurability, there is no time like the present to begin the transition to mass customization.

Is the Mass Customization Journey Worth It?

Discrete manufacturers struggling with business execution and profitability issues need to consider mass customization as a far more effective enterprise-wide business strategy. The reasons for this seem clear:

- Dramatically reduce engineering effort per order configuration
- Create headroom for innovation
- Differentiation
- Connect customer to enterprise
- Increase velocity and reduce burden
- Increase customer satisfaction
- Reduce cycle times
- Create process dependency while eliminating people dependencies

What kind of benefits can be realized?

- Dramatic reductions in cycle times in core business processes—up to 80% or 90% reductions aren't uncommon
- Better factory flow actually creates capacity as manufacturing lead times decrease

- Eliminating the burden of ineffective business processes and enable an organization's ability to efficiently and seamlessly move orders from sales administration through the factory
- Leaning the business—eliminating waste
- Eliminating the cost and risk of finished goods inventories

The journey is worth it!

Closing Margin Leaks

[Note: What follows is a transcript of an executive briefing delivered by Dave Gardner in 1996. The elements of this briefing are timeless.]

Imagine this! You're about 2.5 weeks before the end of your company's fiscal year. The company president has called an urgent meeting of his entire management team.

He starts by telling you that you have a unique opportunity to be *first* in your marketplace, that you *welcome* this opportunity and challenge, and that you will *meet* this opportunity and challenge.

You glance across the room at the other managers assembled, shrug your shoulders a bit, and quickly return your attention to the president, wondering all the while what hair-brained idea you're going to hear about next.

He goes on to tell you that the company will immediately be announcing the highest capacity disk drive ever available in your marketplace.

And, most importantly, your company would be doing this before any of your competitors.

Nobody had a product like this. The company would be taking the market-place by storm.

And, then the real bombshell hits. He tells you that we'll begin shipping this new high-capacity disk drive in 2.5 weeks—just in time for our fiscal year-end shipments.

While many of you might be giddy with excitement over the prospect of such an opportunity, when I heard this, I felt like I had just taken a direct hit from a canon ball that separated me from some of my vital organs.

You see, I was the configuration support manager and I had a really big problem. My department didn't have a 2.5-week process to get the documentation pulled together to support the release of a new product.

Under the best of circumstances, I had, at a minimum, a 4-week process, which, if anybody had checked our actual mileage, was probably running closer to 8 weeks.

So, what could I do?

- I certainly didn't want my department to be the reason we couldn't meet this business opportunity.
- And, somehow, it just didn't seem right to raise my hand in front of all my peers and the senior leadership team and say, "Umm, excuse me, but the process my department uses can't possibly support such an aggressive schedule."

When the president announced that we were going to be shipping this new product in 2.5 weeks, I believe I correctly discerned that that wasn't a hope, a goal, or just something he wanted us to try to do.

This felt more like a commander ordering his troops. This was something we were going to accomplish come hell or high water.

About 25 people left this 3-minute meeting shaking their heads. I'm sure that many of them returned to their offices, closed their office doors, and crawled into the fetal positions underneath their desks. The thought surely crossed my mind.

What the president wanted seemed an impossible task. This crazy guy wanted us to do something almost as ridiculous as running a 3-minute mile.

I stayed after the meeting, walked up to the president, and informed him that I could do my part, but to meet his time objective:

- I would have to implement a radically different approach to describing our company's modular, expandable, "build-to-order" products.
- I told him my approach would streamline and simplify the way we created our top-level product documentation.
- I told him that I had had exploratory discussions with several key individuals in the company about changing the process, but, that people didn't seem interested in the change, they seemed hell-bent on preserving the status quo.

The status quo wouldn't work this time. Without hesitation, and, with a twinkle in his eye, the president looked me square in the eyes and said, "Do it!"

At last, out of sheer business necessity, I got the green light I needed.

But, to heck with the green light I received. Do you have the green light you need?

- Is your company being held hostage to a configuration process that doesn't serve your business needs?
- Does it take too long to get quotes in the hands of customers?
- Do your salespeople sell configurations you can't deliver?
- Does it seem you ship more "specials" than standard orders?
- Are your gross margins slipping?
- Does everyone in your company have the same understanding about the product configuration capabilities of your products?
- Is your top-level product documentation the bottleneck in getting products from product development into manufacturing?

These are just a few of the issues that plague manufacturers of configurable products.

I want to describe a proven solution to deal with these operational issues associated with manufacturing custom, build-to-order systems from a standard selection of system components.

I want to share with you my vision for what's needed, what you are up against, and what choices you have to consider.

So, let's get started.

Margin Leaks

Manufacturers are under tremendous pressure to reduce prices and cut costs in today's competitive, global marketplace. A paradox has emerged creating what I call "margin leaks" for manufacturers.

"Margin leaks" are those insidious, hidden, intangible costs of inefficiency that, for reasons that often defy explanation, keep driving up your cost of doing business and eroding your profits.

Let me repeat that: "Margin leaks" are those insidious, hidden, intangible costs of inefficiency that, for reasons that often defy explanation, keep driving up your cost of doing business and eroding your profits.

How Much Are the Margin Leaks Costing You?

The answer varies—cost estimates range from 1% to 3% of total revenues. This estimate is low. The estimates only look at inefficiencies in the factory, cost of replacing missing parts, and expediting parts shortages.

The cost estimates do not consider the extra time sales and customer service personnel invest with customers, lost selling time, additional travel costs, premium shipping costs, accounts receivable collection delays and costs, and the cost of customer dissatisfaction.

The Source of Margin Leaks

The source of margin leaks lies between our mass production traditions and the "build-to-order" business methodologies required to support customer's demands that they "have it their way."

Current manufacturing systems and practices have their origins in a premise advanced by Henry Ford: "You can have it in any color as long as it's black."

The implication behind Mr. Ford's statement is quite profound: The efficiencies within the factory that reduce your costs and your selling price can't be achieved if you allow any variation in the products you sell to your customers. Variety undermines efficiency and drives cost up.

Can you imagine Ford Motor Corporation being limited to selling black cars? Of course not! They sell many diverse models of vehicles in millions of different configurations yet they are competitive with their rivals.

How, then, can manufacturers offer great variation in their products and contain costs—an unthinkable concept for Henry Ford?

The answer lies outside current solutions employed by manufacturers. Current implementations of methodologies employed by manufacturers are inadequate to support "build-to-order" business strategies.

A quick examination of four common margin leaks provides clear evidence of the problems.

Margin Leak #1: Shipping More "Specials" Than Standard Orders

Most "build-to-order" manufacturers make the mistake of creating a discrete bill of material for each configuration of product that might be sold. To reduce the documentation workload, engineering and marketing meet and agree to restrict the choices that a customer is permitted to make.

Gardner's Law concerning "Number of Bills of Material Required to Satisfy Customer Demand" is

> *There is a need to create "n + 1" bills of material, where "n" is an unknown and very large number.*

It's not possible (or practical) to create a bill of material describing every configuration a customer might want.

"Special" orders occur whenever a customer has a requirement that falls outside the scope of the predefined configuration choices. When this occurs, people throughout the organization scramble like mad to (1) determine if the configuration is technically feasible and, if it is, to (2) create the documentation manufacturing needs to produce the order.

Your customers are sophisticated—they are not content with prepackaged choices. They do not want to pay more than they believe they need to nor will they be satisfied with less than what they want. Customers expect manufacturers to accommodate their need for flexibility and to help them satisfy not only today's needs, but tomorrow's as well.

If you are shipping more "specials" than standard orders, it means that the business process you use to define allowable configurations is (1) not representative of the true flexibility of your product and (2) is defined at too high and discrete a level to satisfy your actual customer demand.

With Margin Leak #1, your costs are

1. Disruptive because the nature of specials creates organizational inefficiency which increases costs.
2. You lose selling opportunities when the customer's actual needs differ from published configurations.
3. Your company creates vast, deep bills of material structures that add to company overhead and do not add any real value to the product.

Margin Leak #2: Giving Away Items the Customer Should Have Purchased Just to Make the Configuration Work

Manufacturers of "build-to-order" products often give away items that should have been purchased because the order has already been accepted. It is too painful for sales to go back to the customer and advise that the cables, power supplies, and cabinets need to complete the installation were overlooked during the sales process.

If your configuration process doesn't allow you to easily identify your customers configuration requirements before you take an order, you will have this exposure. Further, if your process doesn't allow you to easily configure add-on (upgrade) orders, you'll have an additional exposure.

With Margin Leak #2, your cost is products that should have generated revenue are given away.

Margin Leak #3: Inability to Validate a Customer's Requirements

If you don't have a comprehensive means to validate your company's product offerings or capabilities against your customer's requirements, you are at increased risk for margin leaks. Without such a mechanism, it often takes longer to validate requirement than sales or the customer can tolerate. This problem is compounded by time zone differences, rapid changes in features or options, short product life cycles, and the need for quick turnaround on orders; as a result, commitments end up being made that the company cannot fulfill.

With Margin Leak #3, your cost

1. Loses future business due to dissatisfaction created during previous selling situations
2. Has processing delays while the company validates customer requests—disruptions create organization inefficiency

Margin Leak #4: Increasing Accounts Receivable Aging due to Delays in Satisfying Customers

Are you finding it takes long to collect your receivables due to problems in completing the installation or the time it takes to resolve configuration-related problems? This is a common manifestation of problems related to "build-to-order" products.

With Margin Leak #4, your cost is the cost of capital plus the drag on your company's reputation.

There are many more examples that I could cite, but I would rather turn the attention to what you should be implementing.

Customer-Driven Manufacturing

Definition: An integrated business methodology designed around the customer and sales.

Key elements:

- Modular bill of material structure and configuration rules
- Configurator application that supports

  - Quotations
  - Forecasting
  - Order submission
  - Electronic product catalog with specifications

- Business processes
- Training

What are the benefits of this new process?

- The Configurator becomes the "air traffic control" system:

  - Controls the arrival of new products, features, and options as well as the departure of old/discontinued products, features, and options
  - Provided control never available with just a price list
  - Helped everyone understand what "released" really meant

- Engineering created about 20% or less of the documentation that would have been required under the old process:

  - Provided a short list of parts and sub-assemblies required to support the new product
  - Reference assembly drawings were created as aids for manufacturing
  - Engineering efforts were focused on innovation, not creating and supporting documentation and production needs
  - The bull's-eye was well defined from the "get-go"—everybody knew what the target was so we were able to hit the target every time
  - The materials planning organization had an extremely flat bill of material to use as a planning bill of material for each product line. Because everything about our approach relied on modularity, the

same core component used in 10 different applications had exactly the same part number.

- The parts issued against sales orders corresponded to the part numbers in the stock room.

- The employees in system integration and test got the items they needed properly issued with each sales order. They were no longer held up for days or weeks with parts shortages. Build cycle times dropped from weeks to less than a day.

- Top-level product documentation efforts dropped from 160 hours to less than 40. New product lines were sometimes created in less than 8 hours from existing components.

- Accounting had a structure that supported different levels of analysis.

- Products got to market faster because sales could begin selling new products before they were released from engineering, not at the last moment just before release to manufacturing.

- Field service had information about what parts they needed. They could assist customers with add-on/upgrade order planning.

- Everyone in the company had the same understanding about products.

- The number of "specials" dropped dramatically. The configurator helped the team address specials in about 25% of the time than would otherwise have been required.

- Employee morale improved company-wide.

- Best of all, top-level product documentation was never again in the critical path for getting a product released.

What Your ERP System Won't Do

Irrespective of whether a manufacturer has a "build-to-order" product line or not, there are three critical areas of a manufacturing company not addressed by ERP:

1. Product development
2. Engineering documentation and change management
3. Sales

a. Quotes

b. Forecasting

Why is it important to recognize this?

There are gaping holes in the infrastructure of the company not accommodated by the ERP system!

My experience is that most company presidents believe that the only automation they need to run their businesses comes from the ERP system in addition to whatever CAE/CAD tools are required in product development.

As the implementation of ERP systems have evolved, the bill of material has become the only means for describing product requirements and relationships.

Bill of materials are perfect for describing very discrete, predictable, configurations of end-items used in manufacturing customer configurations. I like to think of these items as product modules or features.

What do you do if your company makes custom configurations of end products built from standard modules or features?

> *The last thing you want to do is create a unique bill of material for each permutation and combination of end product.*

Your business is not about hundreds and hundreds of bills of material attempting to describe possible order configurations nor is it about page after page of product trees.

Product trees and bill of materials don't:

- Help sales understand what works with what and what configurations they can sell (nor will they prevent sales from selling configurations that can't possibly be built)
- Help with the problem of forecasting demand for system components
- Help audit the product as it ships
- Help get invoices paid sooner
- Make our Engineering Change Order packages smaller and more coherent

- Reduce the number of "specials"
- Help in understanding product margins

It seems that manufacturers of "build-to-order" products ship product in spite of, and not because of, the product documentation and product structure.

Manufacturers of "build-to-order" products often have two major sources of revenue and, as a result, two challenges:

1. Being able to configure new system orders, if your product is expandable
2. Being able to configure add-on (or upgrade) orders

It is important to recognize these two, distinctly different aspects of this business. Most companies' processes aren't effective in dealing with new system orders. If expandability is a feature of your products, be aware that most systems fail completely in addressing this business need.

How I Discovered a Solution to Configuring New System Orders and Add-On Orders

I began thinking, "Why do we have all these bills of materials to configure products? What does it take to formulate them?"

As I pondered this, I realized two very important things—two things that led to a paradigm shift for me:

1. If someone knew how to create all those bills of materials describing the different permutations and combinations of products, the mere fact that they could do this meant that the bills had to be based on some hidden algorithms or rules.

You know, some simple like, "Gee, every time I add 1 of these parts, I need to add 2 of those parts."

The bill of materials held the secrets—the secrets I needed to break away from the cumbersome, burdensome product structure that concealed (rather than revealed) critical information that people required in order to be able to understand how the product configurations were built.

You see, it wasn't the bills of material that we needed—it was the underlying rules!

2. By having a clear understanding of the rules, and by expressing part requirements in a tabular format, not only could I develop the means to configure new system orders, but also accommodate add-on or upgrade orders with the same product documentation!

No system that I have ever observed could accomplish both of those business objectives! And, what was even more remarkable, for a good many high-technology firms that I worked with, add-on or upgrade orders represented about 50% of a company's total revenue. This was a breakthrough.

These realizations explained why expert systems, which are hierarchical in nature, wouldn't support add-on orders. Secondly, it helped explain why large companies who had opted for expert systems were dying under the weight of the systems.

Please see Appendix B for an example of a Configuration Order Worksheet which identifies elements a customer is buying, and Appendix C identifying the "no-charge" configurable items that are needed to complete the configuration. (Note: This information provides the basis for an electronic product configurator.)

What Steps/Criteria Would I Use in Thinking About Constructing a Tool to Configure End Products?

- Base your overall configuration starting point around how your customers and sales think about or view each product line. You need to define a consistent starting point that will work across a number of products and product lines. Look at the major building blocks of each product line—your price list may offer important clues.
- The more closely you tie the product modularity to the way the customer views what they are buying, the more likely the customer's purchase order will resemble your internal sales order. This is important as it is all too common that the more challenging it is for the customer to match their purchase order to your shipping/order documents, the greater the delay there can be in getting paid.
- Design your product structure to be as flat and modular as possible.

- Make your product structure "add-only" meaning you never remove parts from a configuration only to add others.
- Describe the relationships between the features and options in terms of descriptive rules.
- Base the rules that you create on the technical capabilities of the product line, not current sales policy.
- Determine if expandability is an issue that is important to customers. Do they expand or upgrade current products installed in the field?
- Recognize that, if you going to be installing add-on products in the field at customer sites, field service does not have access to floor stock items (hardware, spacers, etc.) that the manufacturing folks have, so those add-on orders will need special installation kits added to the order for "add-on" orders only. Those kits should always include extra hardware just in case something gets lost or rolls underneath another piece of equipment during the installation process.

  - Phantom (or blow-thru) bills of materials won't work for these kits
  - Any sub-assembly that is a field-replaceable item also can't be a phantom

What Might Customer-Driven Manufacturing Feel Like?

- It would feel like the walls around the different silos within the company have begun to fall away.
- Some of the following feelings might disappear:

  - Engineering always knows better than operations what operations needs
  - Operations never gets what it needs from engineering
  - Products get shipped—often late—in spite of, not because of, the process
  - Departmental infighting

As the former President of Intel Corporation, Andy Grove, said:

There's at least one point in the history of a company where you have to change dramatically to rise to the next level. Miss that moment and you start to decline.

The cost of plugging the margin leaks is a fraction of their annual cost. Manufacturers of "build-to-order" products have special business needs not addressed by conventional processes.

It is possible to design and implement a comprehensive business methodology to plug your margin leaks—I've accomplished this even in situations where clients believed their problems couldn't be fixed.

Your margin leaks don't have to be a cost of doing business.

Configuration Order Worksheet

[ ] New System with Cabinet

[ ] Add-On to Existing Cabinet

1. Cabinet Configurations Supported
For new system orders, select from the following cabinets available.

(Note: Installation is not permitted in cabinets other than these.)

Model No.	Qty	Description
1234	Qty____	60-inch high cabinet, 110 VAC
1235	Qty____	60-inch high cabinet, 220 VAC
1237	Qty____	42-inch high cabinet, 110 VAC
1238	Qty____	42-inch high cabinet, 220 VAC

The 60- and 42-inch high cabinets will support up to a maximum of

60-inch high cabinet	42-inch high cabinet	Product Type
2	1	Disk drive– controller interface
And	and	
8	4	High-capacity disk drives
or	or	
8	4	Really high-capacity disk drives

2. Disk Drive Types and Drive Packages Supported

Select disk drive type and quantity providing they do not exceed the maximum permitted in any single cabinet:

Model No.	Qty	Description
2100	Qty_____	High-capacity disk drive, fixed, 110 VAC
2101	Qty_____	High-capacity disk drive, fixed, 220 VAC
2200	Qty_____	Really high-capacity disk drive, fixed, 110 VAC
2201	Qty_____	Really high-capacity disk drive, fixed, 220 VAC

Configuration Order Worksheet

No-Charge Configurable Item Order Worksheet

1. Internal-to-External Cable Transition Panel

For *New System Orders*, select the appropriate quantities from the table below based on the number of disk drives required by the customer, and specify the items on the lines immediately below the table.

For *Add-On Orders*, subtract the items that are present in the existing customer configuration from the items that would be present in the new customer configuration and specify the net, positive difference(s) on the lines immediately below the table.

Model No.	Number of Disk Drives							
	1	2	3	4	5	6	7	8
3100	1	1	1	1	1	1	1	1
3101	2	2	2	2	2	2	2	2
3102	2	2	4	4	6	6	8	8
3103	0	2	2	4	4	6	6	8
3104	10	10	8	8	6	6	4	4
3105	12	10	10	8	8	6	6	4
3106	2	2	2	2	2	2	2	2

Model No.	Qty	Description
3100	Qty_____	Frame, transition panel
3101	Qty_____	Transition panel
3102	Qty_____	Adapter kit, 60-pin connector
3103	Qty_____	Adapter kit, 40-pin connector
3104	Qty_____	Blank cover plate, 60-pin connector
3105	Qty_____	Blank cover plate, 40-pin connector
3106	Qty_____	Label, configuration

Note: See the following pages for an example of how this would be used.

Assume a "New System Order" requires four Disk Drives:

1. Internal-to-External Cable Transition Panel
For *New System Orders*, select the appropriate quantities from the table below based on the number of disk drives required by the customer, and specify the items on the lines immediately below the table.

Model No.	Number of Disk Drives							
	1	2	3	4	5	6	7	8
3100	1	1	1	1	1	1	1	1
3101	2	2	2	2	2	2	2	2
3102	2	2	4	4	6	6	8	8
3103	0	2	2	4	4	6	6	8
3104	10	10	8	8	6	6	4	4
3105	12	10	10	8	8	6	6	4
3106	2	2	2	2	2	2	2	2

For *Add-On Orders*, subtract the items that are present in the existing customer configuration from the items that would be present in the new customer configuration and specify the net, positive difference(s) on the lines immediately below the table.

Model No.	Qty	Description
3100	Qty_1_	Frame, transition panel
3101	Qty_2__	Transition panel
3102	Qty_4_	Adapter kit, 60-pin connector
3103	Qty_4_	Adapter kit, 40-pin connector
3104	Qty_8_	Blank cover plate, 60-pin connector
3105	Qty_8_	Blank cover plate, 40-pin connector
3106	Qty_2__	Label, configuration

Note: The person configuring this doesn't need to know anything about the parts or do any translation—they simply need to learn to find the correct column and write the numbers onto the form. We had order worksheets available that didn't have all the rules and tables on them so the features could be tallied on a sheet that more easily accommodated order entry.

Assume, an "Add-On" Order Will Upgrade the Configuration from four to six Disk Drives:

1. Internal-to-External Cable Transition Panel
For *New System Orders*, select the appropriate quantities from the table below based on the number of disk drives required by the customer, and specify the items on the lines immediately below the table.

For *Add-On Orders*, subtract the items that are present in the existing customer configuration from the items that would be present in the new customer configuration and specify the net, positive difference(s) on the lines immediately below the table.

Model No.	Number of Disk Drives							
	1	**2**	**3**	**4**	**5**	**6**	**7**	**8**
3100	1	1	1	1	1	1	1	1
3101	2	2	2	2	2	2	2	2
3102	2	2	4	4	6	6	8	8
3103	0	2	2	4	4	6	6	8
3104	10	10	8	8	6	6	4	4
3105	12	10	10	8	8	6	6	4
3106	2	2	2	2	2	2	2	2

Model No.	Qty	Description
3100	Qty_____	Frame, transition panel
3101	Qty_____	Transition panel
3102	Qty_2_	Adapter kit, 60-pin connector
3103	Qty_2_	Adapter kit, 40-pin connector
3104	Qty_____	Blank cover plate, 60-pin connector
3105	Qty_____	Blank cover plate, 40-pin connector
3106	Qty_____	Label, configuration

Note: In this example, we need to ship only quantity 2 each of the 3102 and 3103 parts. The blank cover plates already installed on the transition panel will be removed when the Adapter Kits are installed. As per the instructions for "Add-On Orders," you exclude any items with the order that are "0" or have a negative quantity.

About the Author

David J. Gardner is a management consultant, speaker, author, and principal of mass-customization-expert.com. He has over 30 years experience in the design and integration of innovative business process and information technology solutions for "start-up" as well as established companies. He is known for his pragmatism and track record of achieving results for his clients.

David has extensive experience helping companies implement

- Mass customization (build to order, assemble to order, and engineer to order)
- Configuration management systems (part numbering systems, change management systems, and online document control systems)
- Operations strategies and information technology integration

He has held management and senior management positions in Engineering; Manufacturing; Sales, Marketing, and Customer Service, and Product Management.

He joined Tandem Computers in 1979 where he was responsible for Corporate Documentation Standards for Tandem's highly configurable and expandable computer systems.

In 1983, he designed and implemented a Configuration Guide for Dialogic Systems instituting a process that greatly simplified a complex, modular product such that the field sales organization and international customers could easily define their order requirements. This methodology satisfied the product definition needs of sales, marketing, engineering, manufacturing, customer service, and finance. David also developed what is believed to be Silicon Valley's first "online document control system" providing a means to support change requests, change orders, and part number assignment.

David improved the approach for defining highly configurable products at System Industries in the late 1980s by developing a methodology that not only accommodated "new system" orders but also fully addressed "add-on" orders. This company built modular disk and tape storage systems that could be attached to each computer system ever produced by Digital Equipment Corporation. Sixty percent of the employees used the Configuration Guides as a means to validate and order highly configurable and expandable storage subsystems used widely with Digital's computing systems.

In July 2002, David was recruited by one of the world's largest manufacturers of fire and rescue vehicles as Vice President of Product Management to lead an enterprise-wide change initiative to transition the company from an "engineer-to-order" to a "mass customization" business paradigm to

- Reduce the cost and lead time associated with engineering each vehicle to improve company profitability
- Reduce overall SG&A expenses
- Accurately describe the company's product configuration capabilities to better set customer and dealer expectations
- Provide accurate material and labor costs to eliminate "margin surprises"

This project involved

- Restructuring the bills of material into a modular structure to create a standardized set of options that could be custom-configured into highly customized vehicles.
- Leading the development and implementation of a new configurator system to assist the company's dealers with configuring products and generating configuration-specific specifications and quotations.
- Designing and implementing a decision-costing system to provide an understanding of the labor and materials cost for each unique, quoted configuration and to provide a means to better align pricing with actual costs. This data was integrated with the company's ERP system as well as the configurator.

David is a graduate of San Jose State University (BA) and Santa Clara University (MBA). He is also a member of the Society for the Advancement of Consulting, LLC, and has been Board Approved in the area of "Mass Customization Strategy and Implementation." This approval means that the consultant has worked in a specialized area for a considerable length of time; has provided detailed, documented evidence of success directly from clients in that specialty; and has conformed to the Code of Ethics of the society, serving as a thought leader and exemplar in the profession in general and their specialty in particular.

He can be reached through his Web site:
www.mass-customization-expert.com.

Recommended Happy About® Books

Purchase these books at Happy About
http://www.happyabout.info
or at other online and physical bookstores.

Overcoming Inventoritis

This book helps anyone involved in the innovation process interested in obtaining better returns from resources applied to innovation.

Paperback: $19.95
eBook (pdf): $14.95

42 Rules for Growing Enterprise Revenue

This book will inspire sales, marketing, and business development executives to re-think old strategies and brainstorm new growth opportunities.

Paperback: $19.95
eBook (pdf): $14.95

Additional Endorsements

"Dave has distilled his years of mass customization insights into an easy-to-read guide for what it takes to implement mass customization."
John Higginson, Vice President, Engineering, FUJIFILM Dimatix

"Gardner's work targets a major competitive threat to all mass producers—the inability to customize effectively from product management to customer installation and acceptance and through to ongoing customer support ... and it is critical. His insights demonstrate that embracing and adopting a mass customization capability is key to long run competitive success. He makes his case for the mass customization adopters as 'winners' in our highly competitive world."
Paul Emery, Principal, Paul Emery Associates, LLP (former CEO of System Industries)

"Our User Group of credit card senior operations executives found David's presentation and insights very informative and entertaining. His real life experiences in the mass customization techniques in the manufacturing of fire trucks was chronicled. He offered advice on how some of these same principles could be implemented in mass customization and production in the wide variety of credit cards issued by major banks."
Tony Rakun, VP North America Commercial Sales, Datacard Group

Printed in the United States
147362LV00002B/2/P

9 781600 051463